r and Society
in Britain
1899–1948

Rex Pope

LONGMAN
London and New York

Pearson Education Limited
Edinburgh Gate, Harlow,
Essex CM20 2JE, England
and Associated Companies throughout the world.

Visit us on the World Wide Web at:
http://www.pearsoneduc.com

First published 1991

Set in 10/11 point Baskerville (Linotron)
Printed in Malaysia, CLP

ISBN 0 582 03531 7

British Library Cataloguing in Publication Data
Pope, Rex
  War and society in Britain 1899–1948.
  1. Great Britain. Social conditions, history, 1837–1952
  I. Title
  941.082

  ISBN 0-582-03531-7

Library of Congress Cataloging-in-Publication Data
Pope, Rex.
  War and society in Britain, 1899–1948 / Rex Pope.
    p. cm. – (Seminar studies in history)
  Includes bibliographical references and index.
  ISBN 0-582-03531-7
  1. Great Britain – History – 20th century.
  2. Great Britain – Social conditions – 20th century.
  3. World War, 1914–1918 – Great Britain – Influence.
  4. World War, 1939–1945 – Great Britain – Influence.
  I. Title. II. Series.
  DA566.2.P66 1991
  941.082 – dc20   91–2171
                                                                        CIP

Transferred to digital print on demand, 2004
Printed and bound by Antony Rowe Ltd, Eastbourne

Contents

Acknowledgements

We are grateful to the following for permission to reproduce copyright material:
the Conservative Political Centre for an abridged extract from *A Policy for Housing in England and Wales* (January 1945) by the Conservative Central Committee on Post-War Reconstruction; the Labour Party for an abridged extract from the Labour Party Election Manifesto, 1945, *Let us Face the Future*; the author's agent on behalf of The Estate of the late Sonia Brownell Orwell and Harcourt Brace Jovanovich, Inc for an abridged extract from *The Collected Essays, Journalism and Letters of George Orwell* by George Orwell (Pub. Secker & Warburg, 1968), copyright © 1968 by Sonia Brownell Orwell; Richard Pankhurst, the author's Executor, for an abridged extract from *The Home Front* by Sylvia Pankhurst (Pub. Hutchinson, 1932); the author's agents on behalf of the Estate of J. B. Priestley for an abridged extract from *Postscripts* by J. B. Priestley (Pub. Heinemann, 1940); Syndication International (1986) Ltd for abridged extracts from articles in *The Daily Mirror* 28.5.40, 8.1.41 and 22.1.41.

We have been unable to trace the copyright holder of *Nella Last's War*, eds. R. Broad and S. Fleming, and would appreciate any information which would enable us to do so.

Seminar Studies in History

Introduction

The Seminar Studies series was conceived by Patrick Richardson, whose experience of teaching history persuaded him of the need for something more substantial than a textbook chapter but less formidable than the specialised full-length academic work. He was also convinced that such studies, although limited in length, should provide an up-to-date and authoritative introduction to the topic under discussion as well as a selection of relevant documents and a comprehensive bibliography.

Patrick Richardson died in 1979, but by that time the Seminar Studies series was firmly established, and it continues to fulfil the role he intended for it. This book, like others in the series, is therefore a living tribute to a gifted and original teacher.

Note on the System of References:
A bold number in round brackets (**5**) in the text refers the reader to the corresponding entry in the Bibliography section at the end of the book. If a name follows the bold number, this is an author of a particular essay in a collection. A bold number in square brackets, preceded by 'doc.' [**doc. 6**] refers the reader to the corresponding item in the section of Documents, which follows the main text. Items followed by an asterisk * are explained in the Glossary.

Part One: The Background
1   War and Twentieth-Century Britain

During the twentieth century, Britain has been engaged in numerous military conflicts, not all of them acknowledged as war. Many of these conflicts have been, in the context of British resources, small scale. Most have involved territory under British rule, much of it (but not all) far from Great Britain herself. The impact of such conflicts on individuals or communities may have been acute; the effect on British society as a whole, in many instances, minimal. This book considers the effects of just three wars, all recognised as such: the Second Boer War (1899–1902), the First World War (1914–18) and the Second World War (1939–45).

The wars of 1914–18 and 1939–45 have sometimes been described as total wars, unlimited conflicts involving attempts to utilise the full economic, social and political as well as military resources of the states involved. Though this definition, and the implied contrast with other wars, are misleading (**4, 6**, Marwick in **17**), it is the case that all three wars focused attention on British social, political and economic institutions. All, it has been argued, led to changes in British society. In addition, the two major conflicts of 1914–18 and 1939–45 have been seen as leading to significant changes in the British system of political economy. It is these supposed political, social and economic changes, their extent, nature and degree of permanency, and the debates among historians concerning their importance and their relationship to war, that form the subject matter of the greater part of this volume.

The century opened with Britain at war in South Africa. By the standards of the great confrontations of the later nineteenth and twentieth centuries, this was not a major conflict. Nonetheless it did, from start to finish, involve 450,000 British troops, including a quarter of a million regulars. In spite of early British reverses (notably at Colenso and Spion Kop), the main Boer army was quickly defeated and the sieges of Ladysmith and Mafeking raised. The main objective, the re-annexation of the Transvaal, was achieved by October 1990. Even the brilliant guerrilla campaign to which the Boers then resorted was eventually crushed by overwhelming military force

1

and the harsh but effective policy of compartmentalising the country, using barbed wire and blockhouses, and systematically destroying farms and sweeping non-combatant inhabitants into concentration camps. In these camps, incompetent administration contributed to the deaths of between 20,000 and 40,000 Boers and black Africans. In March 1902, the Boers accepted an armistice and May of that year saw the quite generous Peace of Vereeniging.

British war casualties were not insignificant (5,774 killed in action, 22,529 wounded, 16,000 deaths from disease) but other consequences of the war had a more marked social impact. Revelations about the numbers of volunteers unable to meet the standards required by the army (one in three overall, three out of five in a city like Manchester) reinforced concern about the condition of the imperial race and the consequences of urban life. The outcome was the establishment of the Select Inter-Departmental Committee on Physical Deterioration (**37, 41, 54, doc. 2**).

The war of 1914–18 was on an altogether greater scale. Moreover, although shopkeepers proclaimed 'business as usual', the demands of war were, up to a point, apparent from the start. During August 1914, Parliament accepted the Defence of the Realm Act (DORA) permitting government by regulation, while Kitchener (brought into the Cabinet as Secretary of State for War), recognising that the war would last for years rather than months and that the British would have to fight on land, called for a New Army of seventy divisions. By the end of 1914, the trenches had been established and the first Battle of Ypres had given an indication of the scale of casualties to be expected. 1915 saw the beginning of a U-boat blockade of Britain and continued heavy losses on the western front, particularly in the Battles of Neuve Chapelle, Second Ypres, Aubers Ridge and Loos. A further 200,000 British and Anzac casualties resulted from the disastrous attempt to force Turkey out of the war by the landings at Gallipoli. 1916–17 brought battles and casualties, on an even larger scale but to little effect, on the Somme (60,000 British casualties on the first day, 450,000 in all) and at Passchendaele (Third Ypres) where there were 270,000 British victims. 1917 also saw a dramatic increase in the efforts made by the Germans to cut Britain's sea supply lines. Between February and July, unrestricted attacks by U-boats sank 3.75 million tons of British, allied and neutral shipping and damaged much more. However, from May the convoy system was increasingly adopted and though losses remained heavy they were on a declining trend and were supportable. By the end of 1917, too, revolution had forced Russia out of the war while the United

States had entered it, and the allied counter-blockade of the central powers was inflicting severe hardships on their civilian populations. 1918 saw the restoration of a war of movement. The German advance of the spring was halted at the Second Battle of the Marne. From August to November, the German armies were forced back, suffering a series of crushing defeats. The collapse of Germany's allies, Turkey and Austria-Hungary, and the demoralisation of civilians and military alike, culminating in the sailors' mutiny at Kiel, the abdication of the Kaiser and anti-war and pro-Bolshevik disturbances in late October and early November, forced the Germans to the armistice of 11 November 1918 (**45, 60, 68, 73**).

At the outbreak of war, the British army had a regimental strength of less than a quarter of a million men. By 1918, 5.2 million men had served in the army, over half as volunteers. Of the male population of England and Wales aged fifteen to forty-nine at the time of the 1911 census, 46.3 per cent had been recruited for the army. The figure for Scotland was 41.5 per cent and for Ireland, where the Home Rule issue led to the authorities treading warily, 12.3 per cent. In addition, over 640,000 had served in the Royal Navy and allied services and 291,000 in the Royal Flying Corps/Royal Air Force. Of the total participating, 723,000 (11.76 per cent) were killed and a further 1.7 million (22.27 per cent) wounded. Most of the dead (93 per cent) and wounded (98 per cent) had served in the army where trench warfare took a terrible toll. 15,000 merchant seamen and fishermen were also killed (**72**).

Military mortality was naturally concentrated among young men. Over half a million men aged under thirty were killed in the war, including, in England and Wales, more than one in seven of the age group twenty to twenty-four. Officers, predominantly drawn from the middle and upper classes, suffered higher casualties (15.2 per cent of those who served in the army being killed) than other ranks (12.9 per cent killed). Common sense and contemporary opinion, but not, unfortunately, adequate statistical evidence, suggests that these losses were concentrated among junior officers serving with their men in the trenches (**72**).

The main military impact of the war on civilians was through the threat or actuality of death or injury to relatives, friends or neighbours. The huge casualty lists of the newspapers left no one untouched. In south-east England there was, too, the sound of the guns, heard sixty miles inland at the time of the bombardment that preceded the Battle of the Somme. The war also brought precursors of the direct civilian involvement that characterised the Second

3

World War. Towns on the east coast such as Sunderland, Scarborough, Whitby and the Hartlepools were shelled by German naval vessels. From 1915, London, Norwich and other towns, including some in the west Midlands, were subjected to bombing from Zeppelin airships. From 1917, Gotha and Reisen Giant aircraft were used to bomb London. Casualties, by contemporary or later standards, were slight (1,266 killed in all) but the impact on a vulnerable civilian population was substantial, leading to outbursts of anti-alien hysteria and to experiences and responses more commonly associated with the conflict of 1939–45: blackout, taking shelter in tube stations, spontaneous migration from London (**45, 68, 77**).

Once again, war brought a reminder of the low physical standards of much of the population. Even the cursory five-minute medical inspections, conducted under the aegis of the Local Government Board in 1917–18 (responsibility having been taken away from the War Office), placed 41 per cent of those inspected in Categories C and D (i.e. not likely to be used for combat duties) and considered 10 per cent quite unfit for any form of military service (**72**).

The resource needs of war led to attention, too, to the civilian labour force. The early months of uncontrolled volunteering had cost important war industries like chemicals, explosives and electrical engineering a quarter of their workforces; the metals and mining industries had fared almost as badly, losing one in five of their workers. Vickers' use of 'badging' to protect its skilled workers was one answer. New working arrangements, allowing the breaking down of engineering processes and the employment of semi-skilled labour (dilution) was another. This was agreed with the relevant trade unions and incorporated in the Munitions of War Act (1915). Dilution turned to substitution when, after pressure to volunteer and attesting (1915) had failed to deliver the men the army wanted, conscription was introduced. The Military Service Acts led to increased numbers of men being replaced in the civilian labour force by women. By 1918, the total number of women in paid occupations stood at 7.3 million, a 22.5 per cent increase on the 1914 figure. The numbers in munitions manufacture had multiplied four-fold to 947,000; those in transport six-fold to 117,200. Nearly half a million were in national or local government jobs, a 75 per cent increase on the 1914 figure (**29, 40, 45, 47, 67**).

The Second World War imposed itself even more on the British population. This imposition did not take the form of even larger-scale military forces, though their make-up – including 500,000 women auxiliaries and over one million men in the RAF – was different. Some 6.5 million and women served in the armed and auxiliary services during the course of the war and the strength of these services in 1945 (5.1 million) differed little from the size of Britain's armed forces in 1918. Military casualties, at 264,000 dead and 277,000 wounded, were much lighter and, in the absence of trench warfare, the army's death toll (144,000 out of 3.8 million, i.e. 3.8 per cent) was proportionately less than that of either the RAF (70,000 dead, 5.9 per cent) or the Royal Navy (51,000 dead, 5.5 per cent). The greater impact on the population as a whole was in the extent to which the labour force was mobilised and regulated, in the sheer duration of the conflict, and in the much greater exposure of civilians to bombing and rocket attack, leading to 60,000 deaths and more than 80,000 persons being seriously wounded (Winter in **121**).

Memories of 1914–18 and the anticipated consequences of bombing contributed to a sombre response to the declaration of war in September 1939. There was a realistic, even exaggerated awareness of the hardship that the war would bring. In fact, following the collapse of Poland, little happened on land until the spring of 1940. Then Hitler occupied Denmark and Norway, following this in May with an attack on the Low Countries and France. In less than a month, the British were forced to evacuate 225,000 of their troops (and over 100,000 French) from Dunkirk. By the end of June, the French government had signed an armistice with the Germans (**90,127**). The threat of an invasion of Britain was real. In the summer of 1940, the Luftwaffe sought, as a prelude to a seaborne attack, to destroy British air defences in the Battle of Britain. In late August and early September the Germans came close to success before, in retaliation for RAF raids on Berlin, their attention was turned from the destruction of aircraft, aerodromes and radar installations to the bombing of cities. The blitz was the manifestation of the terror bombing which had been feared. But although in 1940–41 over 2 million houses were damaged or destroyed and 43,000 civilians killed, the burden proved bearable and, as important, the change of German tactics freed Britain from the threat of invasion (**89**).

During 1941, the German armies advanced into south-east Europe and deep into the Soviet Union. Meanwhile, U-boat attacks on British shipping, particularly in the Atlantic, were building up, threatening food and other supplies. Between June 1940 and December 1941, one-third of Britain's merchant tonnage was sunk, three times as much as the country was able to replace from its own yards. The burden in merchant seamen's lives was also a heavy one, 30,000 being killed in the course of the war (**89, 90**).

1942–43 saw the tide turn. The attack on the Soviet Union absorbed the greater part of German military manpower and equipment. Though fortunes on the Eastern Front fluctuated, German losses were heavy and the outcomes of the Battles of Stalingrad (November 1942–February 1943) and Kursk (July 1943) decisive. The aftermath of Pearl Harbor (December 1941) brought the USA, by far the greatest economic power in the world, into formal conflict with Germany, adding to the considerable assistance she had already been able to give Britain through 'Lend Lease' and other means. The Americans managed to halt the Japanese advance in the Pacific, while in North Africa victory at El Alamein and the Anglo-American landings in Morocco (October and November 1942 respectively) were the first steps on the road to the defeat of Germany.

In the Atlantic, German U-boats continued to try and break the supply lines between the United States and Britain. This led to mounting losses of seamen and shipping. In each of the worst months (March, June and November 1942) over 800,000 tons of allied or neutral shipping were sunk. However, by the end of 1942 American yards could build ships faster than the Germans could sink them, and improved allied intelligence, weaponry and tactics were making U-boat losses intolerable. In May 1943, the German Admiral Doenitz abandoned the attempt to conquer the Atlantic. In addition, 1942–43 saw mounting RAF and USAAF bombing raids on German cities and installations. By late 1943, the Russians were moving remorselessly westward. Island-hopping was taking US forces ever closer to Tokyo, and the allied invasion of Sicily and then mainland Italy had led to the Italians' surrender (**89, 90, 127**).

By this time victory was assured, but it was slow in arriving and there were still setbacks and suffering to come. German defences in Italy proved obdurate. There were heavy casualties in the Battle of Normandy following the D-Day landings (June–August 1944). The failure at Arnhem (September 1944) was followed by the German counter-attack in the Ardennes (December). South-east England, and in particular London, was subject to attack by flying bomb (V1) from June 1944 and by rocket (V2) from September, killing over 6,500 people and injuring a further 22,000. Victory in Europe was not achieved until May 1945; victory over Japan (with the help of atom bomb attacks on Hiroshima and Nagasaki) followed in August (**89, 90**).

Second World War governments had the experience of 1914–18

to learn from. Thus Chamberlain's government instituted a Military Training Act (May 1939), replacing it, when war broke out in September, with a National Service Act which imposed eligibility for military service on all men aged eighteen to forty-one. In order to protect key industries, it also introduced a Schedule of Reserved Occupations and a (largely ineffectual) Control of Engagement Order. The real achievements of mobilisation were, however, those of Churchill's coalition government, with Bevin * as Minister of Labour and National Service from May 1940. A series of Acts (1940–42) imposed eligibility for national service, of one sort or another, on all men and women between the ages of eighteen and sixty.

As in the war of 1914–18, normal trade practices were suspended in war-related industries. In 1939, before war broke out, the Engineering Employers Federation and the Amalgamated Engineering Union had agreed to dilution arrangements. Though progress was initially disappointing, the process of substitution or of temporary upgrading of semi-skilled workers was to proceed rather further than it had in the earlier war (**92**).

The overall effect of the mobilisation arrangements was impressive. In mid-1943, when wartime civilian employment was at its peak, it numbered 17.1 million, just 900,000 down on the mid-1939 figure. The 4.2 million men and women lost to the forces since the outbreak of war had been compensated for by natural demographic trends, by the virtual elimination of unemployment and, above all, by the increase from 4.9 to 6.7 million in the number of women in recognised paid employment. Even these figures underestimate quite substantially the total numbers playing some part in the civilian war effort, since they discount half the 750,000 women working part-time plus all those working beyond the age of sixty (women) or sixty-five (men) and those, including the WVS, engaged in unpaid voluntary activity. Within the overall numbers, there was a four-fold increase in those engaged in supplying the forces, from an already-inflated 1.25 million in 1939 to 5.1 million at this mid-1943 peak. During the course of the war, the numbers employed in central and local government also grew (by half a million) as did those in agriculture (by 160,000). Conversely, the workforce of building and civil engineering fell by 52 per cent, that of clothing, boots and shoes by 39 per cent, that of textiles by 37 per cent and that of the distributive trades by 32 per cent (**116**).

The wars, then, of the first half of the twentieth century involved ever larger proportions of the British population to ever greater degrees. These vast conflicts appeared to coincide, both in Britain

7

and abroad with major social, political and economic developments. This has contributed to the growth of a body of historical writing investigating not only the relationship between particular wars and specific aspects of change but also the nature of any general relationships between wars and society.

2 Theories on the Impact of War on Society

Historians investigating the impact of war on society can be divided into those who see wars as a catalyst for change, and those who minimise their effects and stress the continuities in social history. The issue, though, is one of emphasis, with most prepared to acknowledge elements of both change and continuity.

Within these broad classifications, we can observe further distinctions. Some advocates of change lay weight on guided developments, government policies; others, notably Marwick, on the unplanned, unanticipated consequences of war (**16**, Marwick in **17**). Among those identifying policy changes, there are contrasts between those who explain these in terms of national military, economic or political need (**38**), and those who believe war can create a feeling of cross-class solidarity in a nation, or that it can create concern for the less privileged amongst those better off (**124**).

There are similar differences among those who play down war's importance as an agent of positive change. Some, particularly historians of social policy, seek to demonstrate the long-term evolution of policy and the influence of agencies independent of war; others go further, seeing war as hindering rather than advancing change or as widening social differences (Smith in **121**). Others, again, see the effects of war as short term or of limited significance, drawing attention to the ability of established elites or interest groups to frustrate any radical alteration in social structure (**50, 89**).

The starting point for most considerations of the general effects of war on societies is Andreski's notion of a Military Participation Ratio. This essentially Social Darwinian theory, resting on a sociology of elites and masses, saw wartime gains by the less privileged members of society as depending on 'the proportion of militarily utilised individuals in the total population'. The greater the demands of war in this respect, the more the pyramid of social structure would be flattened (**2**).

Richard Titmuss's work related specifically to issues of social policy. Modern war has made ever greater quantitative and qualitative demands on the human resources of countries. This means that governments have had to produce populations fit to fight those wars and have had to cater for the casualties of those wars. With regard to the Second World War, Titmuss also identified a post-Dunkirk solidarity (both spontaneous and promoted), seeing the Beveridge Report and other White Papers on social policy, along with the Labour Party election victory of 1945, as reflections of an increased egalitarianism in public attitudes (**23, 124**).

The most prolific of recent writers on war and society has been Arthur Marwick. His ideas have been refined and developed in a series of works since the 1960s. His 'four-part analytical framework' (not Professor Marwick's choice of description) represents the fullest development of his theories, which appear to work best when applied to democracies engaged in twentieth-century wars (**14, 15, 16**, Marwick in **17**). For Marwick, war is, first of all, destructive and disruptive. Twentieth-century wars, for example, have been destructive of life or disruptive of Britain's education service. Action is required. Invalids and widows have to be cared for; educational disruption made good. War also 'tests' institutions and ideas. These relate not only to military issues but also to matters social, political or economic. Marwick sees new norms of social policy established because existing provision failed the tests of the First World War. Similarly, citing J. M. Winter (**69**), he sees the ideas of Labour theoreticians as being tested and refined during the same conflict.

Participation in war and its relationship to social gains, the area studied by Andreski and Titmuss, constitutes the third element of Marwick's framework of analysis. His approach is broader and subtler. He accepts the view that participation involves civilians as well as the military, and that the qualitative nature of that involvement is important. However, he sees social policy or demostrategy as less important than unguided change, where social levelling results primarily through the operation of supply and demand within the labour market and through the prestige and status acquired by participation. Thus one effect of working-class participation in the Second World War is seen as a change in entrepreneurial attitudes – 'an end to the "hire 'em, fire 'em" mentality of the 1930s'.

The final element of Marwick's framework relates to the social-psychological impact of war. This, he suggests, appears in two forms. It can involve an intensification of 'in-group' feelings and thus enhanced antagonism towards 'out-groups'. As such, it aggravates class divisions. It can also create a mood of excitement, one where change is accepted or even demanded. As with participation, the consequences can be guided, for example, government concern for morale in the face of cynicism or class antagonism in the Second World War. Alternatively, it can be spontaneous, as shown by evidence that people during the Second World War became more politically conscious, better able to articulate their expectations or to recognise the legitimate aspirations of others. Here, however, as in respect of other elements of his thesis, Marwick adds a note of caution – not all changes in government style or popular attitudes prove lasting (**16**).

Before turning to consider contrasting views on the effects of particular wars, or on particular aspects of Britain's twentieth-century history, it is necessary to warn against undue parochialism. War-induced changes in society have not been a uniquely British experience, nor would changes in Britain appear that great to a citizen of Germany, Japan or the USSR. Moreover, it may well be that, with regard to economic matters especially, international developments (for example, changes in patterns of trade or of international indebtedness, the overthrow of European political systems or elites) have been at least as significant for Britain as those which have taken place in this country (**4, 19, 66**).

An issue which has occupied historians for nearly half a century, and one which is central to debates about the permanency of war-induced change, concerns the extent of, and reasons for, the retreat of government in the period following the First World War. That war had seen an expansion of government control and intervention far beyond anything previously experienced or even envisaged. Government controls were introduced piecemeal, which perhaps accounts for their ready acceptance while the war continued. However, for Richard Tawney, writing in the Second World War and seeking to establish the case for continued intervention and controls following that later war, the means by which controls developed was their source of weakness. 'A collectivism had emerged which was doctrineless'; there was no new notion of the nature of the relationship between the state and economic life. Thus controls collapsed at the war's end (**65**).

Tawney assumed that there was a choice. Controls and an enhanced state role might have continued after the war. Philip Abrams, in the field of social policy, agreed. He stressed the extent to which First World War social reformers were deceived by reconstruction rhetoric and failed to recognise underlying divisions that, surfacing after the conflict, wrecked their plans. Abrams also drew attention to the need to identify qualitative distinctions in war participation. This, he argued, explained the limited achievement of

11

the labour movement, as a result of the First World War, and the 'significant' gains of 'middle-aged, propertied' women who had played an active role in the policy-proposing sub-committees set up by the Ministry of Reconstruction (**24**).

Others, P. B. Johnson, Rodney Lowe and Trevor Wilson among them, see the failure to maintain a positive government role as stemming from inappropriate political organisation or a lack of political will. The establishment of a Ministry of Reconstruction, alongside and as a rival to established government departments, proved counter-productive. The Ministry and its advisory committees were energetic in formulating plans but were caught unprepared by an unexpectedly early end to the war, and by the change in parliamentary attitudes which followed the November 1918 'coupon' election*. Though reformers and their policies remained influential until late 1919, an increasingly hostile political and economic climate deprived ministers and officials in interventionist ministries of the will and the sophistication to resist the pressures for retrenchment and economic retreat (**42, 44, 68**).

Others, again, query the extent to which there was a choice or, conversely, whether controls, intervention and reform were, in practice, abandoned. Susan Armitage considers that ongoing government controls were never practical politics; Peter Cline that they ceased to be once Germany collapsed. Businessmen and politicians, though ambivalent or unhappy about a continuing government economic role, were prepared to accept this in the interests of national security. For as long as it appeared likely that Germany would emerge from the war as an economic threat to the allies, continued government controls remained on the agenda. The collapse of Germany and the apparent removal of this formidable economic rival meant the end of any possibility of continued controls (**26**, Cline in **30**).

While most historians acknowledge the difficulty, in an essentially dynamic society, of isolating the effects of war, and while many, including military historians, would argue that the continuities between pre- and post-First World War Britain were more significant than the changes, several writers have, at the same time, drawn attention to the ways in which Britain in the 1920s differed from the Britain of the Edwardian era. There had been a redistribution of national wealth towards the salariat and wage earners and some narrowing of differentials within those groups. Whether through taxation or the desire to take advantage of increased land values, the immediate post-war period had seen large-scale land sales and a further diminution of the social and political influence of the landed classes. Taxation had increased and the proportion of the GNP spent on social services had risen from 4 per cent to 8 per cent. There had been an expansion of educational opportunity and, with it, increased 'white-collar' employment. The principle of state-subsidised housing had been established, as had a national system of unemployment insurance and 'doles'. There had been great additions to the numbers of state pensioners. Though the non-interventionist principles of Gladstonian liberalism had clearly been in retreat prior to 1914, historians such as Marwick, Waites or Trevor Wilson see this 'linked' series of changes as at least influenced and speeded by war (**27**, **45**, **66**, **68**).

Nonetheless, though the war may have brought commitment to, and the actuality of, an improvement in the incomes and social welfare of many members of the working classes, it did not, for these and other historians, bring any government-led re-ordering of society. Gail Braybon stresses the economic setbacks suffered by women in the aftermath of war, with the 1920–22 slump completing the process that the rundown of munitions industries and the attitudes' of employment-exchange officials, press, trade unions and politicians had begun. For Bentley Gilbert, even social policy measures can be interpreted as an attempt to conserve, in the face of the upheaval of war, as much as possible of the old order, or as a continuation of the expansion in state welfare evident in late Victorian and Edwardian times (**29**, **38**, **45**, **66**, **68**).

The motives for changes intended, or brought about, by the First World War are variously interpreted. The demands of war and its impact on the 'rhythms and social patterns of everyday life' (Waites) are generally acknowledged. The disruption took the form of inflation and the curtailment of civil, including employment, liberties. It involved the disruption of normal development, for example in house construction, and an accumulation of potential problems. Over time it led to unrest or the threat or fear of it in the forces and among the civilian population [**doc. 9**]. The war and its sheer scale shocked and horrified people but, for Marwick, it 'mobilised' minds (**45**).

The disruptions of war are claimed to have created an 'irresistible pressure' for the reorganisation of society (Deluge), a sense of community (Wilson) or a resort to nationalism, in Britain as elsewhere, in a quest for security (Waites). A number of historians (**35**, **38**, **66**, **68**) draw attention to the tensions created, the consequent political disturbances abroad and industrial unrest at home. In the later years of the war and in the period which followed, a close watch was kept, by Basil Thomson and what was to become known as the Directorate of Intelligence (and later as the Special Branch), on organisations of industrial workers, on servicemen and on the ex-servicemen's associations. The Out-of-Work Donation and the subsequent extensions in unemployment insurance are seen as a direct attempt to head off unrest (**38**). Englander puts this in the context of a wider apprehension regarding members of the forces. Increasingly, they were seen as a threat rather than as saviours. Unemployment relief went with grants for education and training, for settlement in business or on smallholdings, with emigration assistance or with the rehabilitation of the disabled in a bid to buy goodwill. Even the provision of demobilisation clothing resulted from the fear of post-war disorder; it was an attempt to get men out of uniform as quickly as possible (**35, 36**).

The fact that the war was principally against Germany, along with the need to maintain the support of the domestic population, and of our allies, for that war, provided further forces for change. Germany had long been seen as a model as well as a threat. In new technologies, in industrial organisation, in education, in social security, it was seen as necessary to identify and make good Britain's perceived deficiencies (**45**). The fact that the war was presented as one of British democracy against Teutonic autocracy meant an accompanying commitment to the elimination of injustices in our own society; such war objectives were also reassuring to allies suspicious that Britain was seeking to further her imperial ambitions (**68**). For Bernard Waites, this stress on nationalism and on the role of the state as the major source of national unity offers an important corrective to a traditional over-emphasis on mentalities and attitudes (**66**).

The nature and importance of mentalities and attitudes is also a central issue in debates concerning the effects of the Second World War on British society. Angus Calder sees the circumstances of war, with the muting of Parliament, the obvious inadequacy of local government, the armed forces encouraging conscripts to think about and discuss their future, and full employment destroying economic sanctions, as creating 'a ferment of participatory democracy' in which ordinary people adopted their own leaders and objectives, including a radically transformed post-war world. For a time, the need to maintain commitment to the war effort meant government concessions to popular demands. But the efforts of the population led to increasing military success, and with it the survival of wealth, bureaucracy and privilege. A new state-linked capitalism and the economic hegemony of the United States, both in large measure products of the war, reinforced the forces opposing popular democracy. For Calder, the later years of the war and the post-war period restored the establishment's traditional practices of 'manoeuvre, concession and studied betrayal'. The post-war Labour government served this process. Attlee was no revolutionary. Calder is prepared to accept Anthony Howard's observation that 'the overwhelming Labour victory of 1945 brought about the greatest restoration of traditional social values since 1660' (**89**, Howard in **119**).

Arthur Marwick, like Calder, sees this war as forcing itself on ordinary people, middle class and working class, and as being accompanied by a steadily developing popular radicalism. There was a faith in a future which people would create for themselves, less dependence on official action or the promises of politicians. Marwick does not deny that existing elites resisted the pressures for change, or that several of the post-war Labour ministers reflected their upper-class backgrounds in their attitudes. However, he rejects Calder's implication of a revolution betrayed. War brought higher living standards and a Labour victory in 1945 that would have been unlikely in 1940. Whatever the failings of that government, the post-war world did see a change in relationships between the classes. For the working classes, work or maintenance became not hopes but assumptions. The industrial and political consensus of the mid-1940s 'was far more humane and genuinely democratic than the attitudes of industry, government and the civil service in the 1930s'. The Labour government was, in many of its actions, actually ahead of this consensus. Post-war social policy, characterised by universality rather than by a stigmatising means test, and the 'new baseline' of enhanced status for women, are seen as representative of a 'people's peace' to follow the 'people's war' (**108**).

A slightly different, but similarly positive, interpretation of the effect of war on society is offered by Paul Addison. Like Waites, he lays emphasis on patriotic or nationalist inputs to change rather than those based on a heightened class consciousness. Indeed, in contrast to Calder and Marwick, Addison sees change as emanating from a radicalised minority among the middle classes. This is the view, too, of Englander and Mason, whose study of the armed forces emphasises the unpolitical nature of the rank and file among the troops, far more concerned with issues such as pay, shortages, the fidelity of wives and girlfriends or with future jobs and security, than with any schemes to change society. Essentially, Addison sees the war as contributing to a convergence of political opinion, with

15

Conservatives forced to accept some of Labour's most important demands. The Coalition government is, for Addison, the representative of a new purposeful and positive consensus aiming to secure social betterment but within a capitalist or mixed economy. The measures of the post-war Labour government and the development of the Conservative Industrial Charter (1947) with its commitment to full employment, social security and strong central guidance to the economy, represent the continuation of this process in peacetime (**80, 95**).

Thus Addison and Marwick share a view of radical but not revolutionary change as a result of war – though for Addison this is led from above, rather than the outcome of irresistible popular demand. Addison also shares Marwick's view that the post-war Labour government was in some ways ahead of popular opinion. Indeed, middle-class rejection of constraints on individual liberties, and the extent to which working-class realities diverged from the social reformers' ideals of citizenship, were first to curb and then reverse the process of change in society (**81**).

Other writers are less convinced that change, temporary or lasting, occurred or that, if it did, it could be attributed to any enlightening effect of war. The interpretation of evacuation, for example, offered by both Macnicol and Crosby, challenges Titmuss's assertion that the Second World War saw the emergence of an ideological consensus on rights and welfare. For these writers, exaggerated and inaccurate accounts of the condition and behaviour of a minority of child evacuees and their mothers probably strengthened a Conservative middle-class and Whitehall conviction that the poor could not be helped by a welfare state. The evacuees were seen as representative of an 'incorrigible underclass of personally inadequate cultural orphans'. The experience of evacuation is seen as similarly broadening social divisions when viewed from the working-class perspective. Besides intruding, with sometimes most unfortunate effects, on the solidarity of working-class family life, the lifestyles and attitudes encountered in reception areas brought home to the evacuees the full extent of economic inequality and middle-class privilege (**91, 103**, Macnicol in **121**).

Most writers on women's experience are also sceptical as to the extent of change. They see the war as leading to more debate than real progress. Equal pay did become a serious issue, but the government continued to insist on discrimination with regard to its own employees. Gender-based thinking continued to characterise the trade unions. Domestic responsibilities remained the 'paramount and private' task of women, thus establishing the dual burden of domestic and outside paid tasks for the working wife. At the same time, concern with population led to measures, encouraged by Beveridge, to make the role of housewife more attractive. Delays in providing day nurseries, and the rapidity with which they were run down at the end of the war, were further evidence of an ongoing disapproval of the working mother. Though women were not driven out of employment at the end of the Second World War and the age structure of the female labour force was changed, patterns of employment remained very much those which had been developing in the inter-war years: there had been no 'revolution in values' (Summerfield in **17**, **118**, Smith in **121**, **123**, **128**, **141**).

Other writers on social policy lay emphasis on continuity, sometimes in spite of the war. For Daniel Fox, the National Health Service was the result of four decades of developing consensus as to how medical care ought to be organised and delivered. The wartime Emergency Medical Service was a product of this process. The belief in medical equity which the NHS was held to symbolise was not a product of the war, and certainly not of the Beveridge Report. Indeed, the essential similarities which Fox sees in the health arrangements of different western nations undermine the arguments for war's importance in shaping Britain's health scheme (Fox in **121**).

Similarly, Deborah Thom sees the 1944 Education Act and its implementation as based on a meritocratic ideology well-established in pre-war years. Such changes in education as did take place were in spite of, or hindered by, wartime conditions. Class differences in education remained; there were those who went to the grammar schools and those who did not. Parents and local authorities conspired to maintain the essentials of the educational status quo (Thom in **121**).

All this is in sharp contrast to the views of Correlli Barnett who argues that, to Britain's long-term disadvantage, the Second World War did lead to a new consensus, articulated by established elites in and out of government, that the social amelioration of the mass of the population should be the principal object of policy. These 'New Jerusalem' policies, designed to make provision for the masses in education, health and social security, were developed without any sense of a limit to financial resources. Through the media, the reformers pursued the analogy of war in planning to tackle the problems of peace, but failed to recognise the extent to which Britain had borrowed her way to military success. By concentrating on meeting popular demand, regardless of resource implications, the wartime coalition was not only pursuing a fantasy but, in doing so, was neglecting to adopt strategies which would transform Britain's obsolete industrial culture (**82**).

This example of 1980s thinking offers a useful bridge to the final contribution to the debate on the effects of the war of 1939–45 to be examined in this chapter. In words reminiscent of Tawney, Jose Harris sees the sense of social solidarity, engendered by the war, as artificial. The war did not produce ideas which could adequately underpin a thoroughgoing social reconstruction. The welfare state was established without a clearly defined notion of welfare or a coherent theory of the state. For some time after the war this was not a problem. However, in the longer term, this later version of Tawney's 'doctrineless collectivism' was to 'be vulnerable to changes in the economic and political climate and to attacks from more rigorous and dogmatic intellectual rivals' (Harris in **121**).

Thus we are left with a number of questions. Insofar as these wars were accompanied by social changes, were these the consequences of war itself or of other forces in a dynamic society? Did any changes prove lasting, and if not, why was this the case? Were any changes the product of domestic circumstances or of developments resulting from, or assisted by, war's impact on the wider world? Did the wars lead to enhanced social solidarity or did they aggravate social divisions? If war influenced social policy, was this because attention was focused on unacceptable social deprivation and injustices, or because war caused a sense of common concern, or because it created or drew attention to the nation's needs, or because welfare measures or promises were a means of maintaining morale, commitment and public order? Indeed, was social policy, the conscious action of government, as important as spontaneous unguided developments – for example in income differentials or employment prospects – in any alteration of the relationships between different sectors of society? Have these wars made any lasting impact on the self-confidence of, the opportunities for, or the status of women? If changes there were, did they stem from the state, or from established elites, or from the creation, by war, of self-conscious and politicised mass-populations? Were any changes revolutionary, radical or marginal? Finally, are we over-concerned to identify change? Were not continuities the more marked characteristic of the periods before and after Britain's wars during the first half of the twentieth century?

Part Two: War and Social
Change in Britain

3   Popular Experiences, Attitudes and Expectations

The Boer War

The Boer War, for obvious reasons, did not impinge on British society to anything like the degree of later wars. Nonetheless, it did demand and achieve the augmenting of the regular army through volunteers. This, along with the contemporary popularity of jingoistic music hall songs, the spontaneous celebrations associated with the relief of Ladysmith or Mafeking, the disruption of pro-Boer meetings by 'jingo mobs', and the Unionist success in the 'Khaki Election' of the summer of 1900, has been seen as evidence of strong support for imperialism by at least a substantial section of the working classes (**41**, **52**, **54**).

In fact, working-class recruitment to the army tended, as usual, to relate more to the state of employment than to any imperial vision. It was greatest in the winter months when many trades were slack and in the later years of the war when unemployment was rising and real wages falling. Early enthusiasm for the war was more marked among the middle classes. Music hall songs, too, are a doubtful source. They were commercial products *for*, not *of*, their working-class audiences, and the sentiments expressed – for example in the popular 'Miner's Dream of Home' – hardly indicated a commitment to imperial adventure. The reliefs of Ladysmith and Mafeking did excite spontaneous rejoicing [**doc. 1**]; they represented honour restored or surprisingly good news at a time when the war was going badly. The aftermath of these events, the rioting jingo crowd, like the disruption of pro-Boer meetings, seems, however, to have been organised by representatives of the middle classes, with medical students prominent in several places. By contrast, most organisations of working men, the clubs or the trade unions, while they provided volunteers and celebrated their safe return, saw the war as a capitalist adventure and were predominantly pro-Boer. Similarly, the 1900 election results reflected Liberal disorganisation, long-term trends in working-class voting behaviour or response to particular local issues; they offer no evidence to support a general working-class vote in support of imperialism or the war (**52, 54**).

The First World War

The First World War began amid widespread, though not universal, enthusiasm and with the popular misconception that the conflict would be short-lived. A war with Germany at some time had been anticipated but its eventual coming, at the beginning of August 1914, was something of a surprise. Indeed, British attention, as events in Europe unfolded during July, had been focused on a rapidly deteriorating situation in Ireland. The approach of war coincided with the August Bank Holiday, Monday 3 August. A large crowd gathered in Trafalgar Square, shouting 'Down with Germany' and singing patriotic songs as the 11 p.m. deadline, set by the British for German withdrawal from Belgian territory, approached. The actual declaration of war, from the Foreign Office, was welcomed with 'round after round of cheers' (**45**).

There *was* opposition. On 2 August, Keir Hardie, H. M. Hyndman, George Lansbury and Arthur Henderson addressed a Labour Party demonstration against war. A Neutrality Committee was established, including the prominent scholars Gilbert Murray and Basil Williams, Ramsay MacDonald (Chairman of the Parliamentary Labour Party) and a number of prominent Liberals. On the 3rd, Hardie, who had worked to create an international socialist movement that would refuse to participate in a capitalist war, threatened united opposition by the workers of the country. On the evening of 4 August, Mrs Fawcett of the National Union of Women's Suffrage Societies was the main speaker in a women's protest meeting against war held in London's Kingsway Hall while, on the same day, the anti-German demonstrators in Trafalgar Square had competition from those opposing war. The Liberal *Manchester Guardian* and *Daily News* also opposed the war – with the latter (rather belatedly on 5 August) carrying a full-page anti-war advertisement, paid for by a body calling itself 'The Neutrality League'. Three Liberal government ministers, Burns, Morley and Charles Trevelyan, resigned over the issue (**45, 68**).

Opponents of war were, though, in a minority. On 6 August, Hardie was shouted down at a peace meeting in his own constituency. Most hostility to war was, moreover, quickly transformed into a grudging acceptance of the need to win and, for many, into a positive enthusiasm for a just war. The Labour Party declared its support for the war and Ramsay MacDonald, who maintained his anti-war stance, had to resign as Chairman of the parliamentary party. Even John Clifford, who had been a leader of pacifist opposition to the Boer War and had returned only recently from a conference of the Churches Peace Alliance in Germany, came to see the war as a religious duty, given Britain's supposed attempts to avert conflict and the Germans' long-planned aggression and flouting of Belgian neutrality (**45**, **68**).

For all the shopkeepers' talk of 'Business as Usual' – a slogan which, initially at least, was eagerly taken up by government – the war brought a substantial degree of economic dislocation. While some industries, such as bootmaking and woollen cloth, benefiting from army orders, experienced a boom, the late summer of 1914 saw a sharp increase in unemployment, even among male skilled engineers, which helped provide the initial volunteers for Kitchener's armies (**60**).

Women's employment was particularly hard-hit. Many servants were dismissed and the sharp fall in the demand for luxuries led to huge lay-offs of women from the dressmaking, millinery and jewellery trades. It was estimated that 44.4 per cent of all women in the paid labour force were unemployed at some time or other during September 1914. The Queen Mary's Fund and the associated Queen Mary's Workrooms, administered by the Central Committee for Women's Employment, a labour organisation, were attempts to provide work (for example, sewing) and subsistence (10s. – 50p – a week in the sewing workrooms) for unemployed women to save them having to turn to charity or to poor relief (**29**, **31**, **77**).

The recruitment of a million young men into the forces by the end of 1914, and the demand for military supplies, led to some improvement in women's job prospects during late 1914 and the first half of 1915. Much of this employment was in areas of military supply, for example shell-filling, where women had always worked, or in non-industrial work in transport, banks or shops – where they sometimes took the place of fathers, husbands or brothers. Trade-union resistance, based on a fear that female employment would reduce the job security and wage levels of their members, hindered further advance (**29**).

During 1915, the Shells and Fuses Agreement between the Engineering Employers Federation and the engineering unions, and the Treasury Agreement between the government and unions (later incorporated into the Munitions Act), opened the way to a sharp increase in women's employment. In 'controlled' establishments, essential to the production of munitions, the principle of dilution of labour was to be accepted. For the duration of the war, skilled men were to work on skilled processes only; semi-skilled employees, including women, could be used as substitutes on other operations (**29, 45, 68**).

Dilution and substitution [**doc. 5**], along with a huge increase in the demand for munitions, accelerated the movement of women into the engineering and explosives industries. This process was further advanced by the introduction of military conscription for males in 1916. Many of the jobs involved repetitive work for which women were supposedly well-suited. Increasingly, though, women were able to demonstrate abilities which allowed them to take on more skilled work. This, in turn, allowed the government to reduce skilled male workers' immunity from military conscription; from February 1918, all male munitions workers aged twenty-five or under were liable to be called up into the forces (**29, 40**).

Women replaced men, too, in industries such as grainmilling, brewing, building and even shipbuilding. Higher pay tended to lure women away from traditional occupations in domestic service, cotton textiles or the clothing industry, leading to an acute labour shortage in these areas. By 1917, London dressmakers were being driven to propose shorter and more regular hours in order to retain their employees.

It would be wrong, however, to overstate the extent or significance of the changes in women's role in the labour force. It was in the interests of governments seeking to encourage further participation, and of feminist organisations demanding improved political and economic status, to exaggerate the role women were playing. Many of those taking up jobs in munitions had transferred from other employment, perhaps a quarter coming from domestic service. Others were married women – sometimes soldiers' wives to whom certain employers gave preference – with previous experience in industry and now needing to return to work. Very few were from the middle classes; the idea that the classes were brought together in wartime munitions work was, by and large, a press and public opinion myth. Nor was the increase in women's employment securely based. By 1917, according to the government's *Labour Gazette*, one in every three women in employment was replacing a male worker. Many of these posts would, under the industrial agreements made, revert to men once the war was over. Nearly a million women were employed in the temporarily expanded munitions industries;

even in early 1918 women were already being laid off from this sector. Those older women who, attracted by better pay, had moved into munitions from industries such as cotton weaving found that they were, in many instances, replaced by girls (Reid in **17, 29**).

Attitudes to women workers remained, in many instances, negative. To skilled men, they were a threat in both the long and the short term. While the war lasted, the ability of women to take on what had been known as men's work meant that increasing numbers of males were vulnerable to military conscription. In the longer term, because men's traditional protection of skill or workplace practice had been undermined, it was feared that women would be used as a weapon in the battle between capital and labour. They had always been a docile, unorganised and cheap labour force; employers were not trusted to honour promises to restore men to their former positions. Though women's experience varied widely, with some women doing skilled work and having the full co-operation of male employees, many were restricted to less-skilled operations and were the victims of hostility and even of sabotage (**29, 47, 78**).

Trade-union views reflected contrasting attitudes of different sections of the male workforce. Thus the Workers' Union and the General and Municipal Workers' Union continued to recruit women members, the former's female membership growing from 4,000 to 80,000 between 1914 and 1918. Some, including the Electrical Trades Union and the National Union of Railwaymen, recruited women for the first time. Others, including craft societies such as the Amalgamated Society of Engineers and the Amalgamated Society of Carpenters and Joiners, or those representing Lancashire cotton spinners, resolutely refused to admit women as members (**29, 31**).

Employers too, partly through preference and partly for fear of upsetting male workers and disrupting production through industrial disputes, were also often reluctant to employ women. Farmers went to great lengths to retain male workers. Many would-be female volunteers could not find work in agriculture. In spite of the formation of the Women's Land Army, there were only 23,000 more women working on the land in 1918 than there had been in 1914. In evidence to the Reconstruction Committee on Women in Industry, employers criticised women for bad timekeeping (in the chemical industries); for inferior workmanship and as incapable of supervisory functions (china and earthenware). They were considered to have only two-thirds the value of male workers in munitions. In Liverpool, union hostility forced women out of dockwork. In cotton-spinning, though women were employed in several towns, against the wishes of the male spinners' unions, as piecers, employers would not use them as spinners; in Preston, the men's union succeeded in keeping women out of the spinning rooms altogether (**29, 47**).

There is evidence, too, that women themselves accepted a subordinate place in the labour market. The National Federation of Women Workers made an agreement with the Amalgamated Society of Engineers, undertaking to withdraw its members from 'men's jobs' as soon as the war ended. Prominent members of the NFWW, disregarding the needs of the single woman or of many working-class wives, espoused arguments that the health of the nation's mothers, and thus of future generations, was put at risk through female industrial employment.

The attention given by press and politicians to women's employment is further evidence of a fundamentally unchanged attitude. There was a patronising wonder at the things women achieved. Neville Chamberlain could speak of women fulfilling their many and diverse new roles 'with an efficiency which had surprised and delighted the whole nation', and a *Daily Mail* journalist wrote of women engineers 'overalled, leather-aproned, capped and goggled – displaying nevertheless woman's genius for making herself attractive in whatsoever working guise'. Even more obviously indicative of unchanging attitudes was the resentment at the high earnings and the conspicuous spending of young female munitions workers ('munitionettes') and the criticism of their independent and sometimes boisterous behaviour (**29, 68**). Nor did war change the attitude of many middle-class women towards entering paid employment, though the loss of domestic servants did, it was claimed, increase the burdens on them [**doc. 7**].

There is no doubt that labour demands during the war brought about an improvement, both absolutely and relatively, in the pay of women and other traditionally low-paid groups. Reid, in particular, argues that there has been a tendency to exaggerate the extent to which this happened. The 14 per cent narrowing of wage-rate differentials between skilled and unskilled in engineering, between 1914 and 1918, has attracted greater attention than the more typical 7 per cent in the coal-mining industry or in shipping (Reid in **17**). Women in munitions work were earning over £2 a week, and women in other industrial work about 25s. (£1.25), by 1918. This compared to an industrial average of 11s. 7d (63p) a week – and about 9s. (45p) a week in the worst-paid industrial occupations – on the eve of war, but it did include substantial overtime payments. Nor did women cease to experience discrimination in pay. There were, in the initial agreements between the state, the employers and the unions, no guarantees of equal rates to women, except to those few who could claim to be doing the job of a fully-skilled tradesman. Indeed, a few days after the Treasury Agreements, the Engineering Employers Federation advised its members that women put on any skilled or semi-skilled parts of a craftsman's job were to be paid at the district rate for youths, not that for adult men. The £1 a week minimum for women in munitions work which was not customarily that of skilled males often, in 1915–16, became the norm. Although there was some progress towards equal piece and time rates for women doing some of the jobs normally undertaken by skilled men, loopholes remained and women continued to be paid at levels below those of males. Indeed, outside munitions, women's wages at best barely kept pace with the increase in the cost of living (**29, 45**).

There are great difficulties in estimating, with any accuracy, changes in relative or real earnings, not least because of wide sector and regional differences. However, it is a fair generalisation to state that wage rates rose quite slowly in the early years of the war, perhaps 10 per cent in each of the years 1914–15 and 1915–16. The year 1916–17, though, saw a 30 per cent increase and 1917–18 an increase of the order of 40 per cent. Thus wage rates were on average, by the end of the war, approximately double the levels of 1914. These figures, though, hide wide sector variations, the extent of changes in overall earnings and changes in the purchasing power of those earnings [**doc. 9**].

By 1917, when wages as a whole had risen some 55 per cent above 1914 levels, those in the cotton industry had only risen by 14 per cent. Bricklayers and painters, also affected adversely by the war, had also experienced relatively low increases. Conversely, agricultural workers had experienced an increase of 89 per cent. Even in 1918, at a time when the cost of living was 110 per cent higher than in 1914, earnings of building workers were only 71 per cent higher and those of coalminers or railwaymen 95 per cent higher than four years previously. Though wage rates for agricultural workers and for unskilled engineers had just kept ahead of inflation with increases of 126 per cent and 113 per cent respectively, those for skilled engineers (73 per cent) and cotton workers (57 per cent) had not (**66, 72**).

How, then, had working-class households been affected by these changes in wage and price levels? Initially, many were hard-hit, especially in areas where substantial numbers had been employed in the service industries or in the manufacture of inessential consumer goods. The opening months of war saw a rapid rise in food prices at a time of widespread under- or unemployment. In Bethnal Green, East London, three times as many needy schoolchildren were receiving free school meals as in the equivalent period in 1913. Eleven per cent of these children were 'military cases', victims of the niggardly level and tardy payment of soldiers' dependants' allowances. Working-class music halls were also hit, one London chain of twenty halls losing £10,500 in the opening three weeks of the war (**31, 60, 68, 77**).

Over time, though, labour became scarce and wages began to rise, but until 1917 they lagged behind prices. Food prices, for example, rose 100 per cent during 1914–17, much more than wages and much more than the Ministry of Food's estimate of a 60 percent increase in the expenditure of a working-class family on food. Fuel prices also rose, by perhaps 2s. (10p) a week for the average family between 1914 and 1918. Clothing was scarce and, though there is evidence of many families cutting back in their spending, nonetheless essential outlay probably added some 4s. (20p) a week to working-class budgets. Among non-essentials, alcohol and tobacco prices rose steeply, though cuts in spending on alcohol appear to have been offset by extra outlay on tobacco (**66, 72**).

Against these increases and working-class changes in expenditure patterns, there were other factors working to protect and enhance the living standards of the bulk of the population. The Rent and Mortgage Interest (Rent Restriction) Act of 1915, introduced in response to agitation on Clydeside, has been described as a major contribution to improving the standards of working-class life (**72**). Rate, fare and insurance contributions all rose very little during the war period. Most important, however, was the extent to which people moved from lower to higher paid jobs, and the way in which additional members of families, women or boys, were drawn into paid employment. When this is put beside opportunities for overtime (ten hours a week average for males in the latter part of the war), the regularity of employment and the fact that there were relatively greater gains for the poorest of the population, we can begin to understand the indicators of rising living standards which accompanied the war (**66, 72**).

Infant mortality continued the decline evident since the turn of the century. Taking 1911–13 as 100, the index of infant mortality fell to 95 in 1914 and 1915, to 82 in 1916, but rose to 87 in 1917 and 1918 (**72**). Overcrowded and inadequate housing and long hours in industrial work may have led to increased mortality from tuberculosis or respiratory diseases but, overall, the war years saw a fall in the adult death rate among civilians. Though the initial effect of war had often been to increase the evidence of poverty, in the longer term the impact was very different. In Bristol, the number of schoolchildren requiring free meals fell sharply from 1,445 on the last day of March 1915 to 114 on the equivalent day in 1916. The Board of Guardians reported a corresponding fall in pauperism in the same city (**68**). In Glasgow, the numbers of schoolchildren reported as ill-clothed and underfed rose from 204 to 264 between 1913–14 and 1914–15 but thereafter fell to 68 by 1916–17 (**45**).

The immense scale of the new armies meant that the military imposed itself, in unprecedented ways, on the daily lives of a large section of the population, and that the relationship between the armed forces (in particular the army) and society was thereby altered. During the first winter of the war, before the army's hutting programmes were properly underway, some 800,000 men were lodged in public buildings or in people's homes. For those in private houses, there were, for many soldiers and hosts alike, all the fears, stresses and petty antagonisms that were to be endured, by perhaps even larger numbers over longer periods, during the Second World War (**27**, **60**).

For recruits, particularly those from middle-class backgrounds, the initial experience of army life – its hardships, its discipline or the ways of new-found colleagues – could be profoundly disturbing (**27**, **60**). For the army, too, there was a need to adjust. Both officers and other ranks were recruited from a much wider cross-section of the population than had been the case in peacetime. Individual indiscipline (including desertion) remained a problem throughout the war. At times, in Britain and in France, this boiled over into group defiance of military orders. However, such occurrences (for example the Soldiers' Councils of 1917) revealed that the men's grievances were essentially over bread-and-butter issues – accommodation, food, allowances, leave or, after the war, early demobilisation. As in the Second World War, the volunteer and conscript army never ceased to see itself as one of civilians temporarily in uniform. While, in the later conflict, this was to cause military leaders some concern, it can be argued that such attitudes contributed to the maintenance of morale in the British army during 1917–18 and also to the absence of any revolutionary political movement at the war's end. The temporary servicemen had retained their identification with elements of the existing civilian order; they failed to develop a servicemen's view. In addition, though millions fought in Britain's First World War armies, the experience seems to have had little lasting influence either on attitudes towards the army (British labour, for example, remained essentially hostile to it) or on the constitution and ideology of the army itself (**27, 36**).

The war led, temporarily at least, to a number of changes in relations between the sexes. In many cases, adult males were conscripted into the forces and women were left to augment family income and single-handedly to manage households. While some writers have suggested that management within the home had always been the female prerogative, others stress the liberating effect of such responsibilities (**68, 78**). The challenge to the myth of male work skills, resulting from women's experience and achievements, particularly in engineering work, served to undermine masculine assumptions of authority outside the workplace. The absence of menfolk and the availability of ready money led to women being seen out together much more than before, not least in public houses (**45, 68, 78**).

The war appeared, too, to lead to rather freer sexual relationships. Certain traditional upper-class constraints, including chaperoning, broke down. The cheapening of life, it has been suggested, contributed to a hedonism which included sexual liberty. There were press outcries at the numbers of single women expecting 'war babies' in areas of the country where large numbers of troops had been stationed, and at the supposed immorality of WAACs stationed in France. Over the period of the war, in spite of a wider knowledge and availability of artificial methods of contraception, the illegitimacy rate rose by 30 per cent. The number of divorces made absolute rose from 596 (1910) to 1,629 (1920). However, too much should not be made of this evidence. Arrangements for paying dependants' allowances to members of the forces revealed that, among the working classes, 'common law' marriage had been far more widespread than had been suspected. The official marriage rate for England and Wales hardly suggests any rejection of traditional values. It had risen from 15.0 to 15.7 per thousand women aged fifteen to forty-four between 1910 and 1914, but leapt to 19.4 per thousand in 1915 before falling back to levels below the 1914 figure during the remaining war years. The rise in illegitimacy was probably, in large measure, no more than a reflection of the obstacles presented by war to the common practice of post-conception legitimising through marriage. Press campaigns were based on limited evidence and are perhaps most revealing as evidence of continuing double standards: the supposed moral laxity of the WAACs was a subject of concern; not that of the British soldiers with whom they were presumed to consort (**45, 60, 68, 72**).

The end of the war coincided with what appeared to be radical changes in the British electoral system. The electorate was extended from eight million to twenty-one million through a sharp reduction in the residential qualifications for the vote and the enfranchisement, with a few largely temporary exceptions, of all males over the age of twenty-one and of six million women over thirty years of age who were either householders, or who were married to householders or university graduates. This was accompanied by a major redistribution of seats and by a reduction in the right to plural voting. By separate legislation, women were allowed to stand for Parliament. In the election which followed close on the armistice, the Labour Party (if we exclude Sinn Fein who refused to take their seats) emerged as the major parliamentary opposition to the government, a position on which the party was able to build in subsequent elections (**31, 45, 68**).

The war had played a part in the democratisation of the franchise and the rise of political labour. War service had meant that most members of the forces, and many civilians, had lost their residential qualification for voting. Thus the government needed to make some change in the law regarding the franchise and had the opportunity to introduce long-demanded extensions and simplifications. In addition, the state had made demands, notably in the form of conscription, of many adult males who had not previously held the right to vote. Natural justice demanded that full political rights be extended to them, a principle reflected in the extension of the vote to men under the age of twenty-one who had experience of active service (**48, 66, 68**).

There is little evidence that war service caused a change in attitudes towards women's political rights. Opponents of the female franchise, like Asquith, appear to have been ready to concede defeat in 1914, but war had delayed progress. The 1916 Speaker's Conference on electoral issues, unanimous on most recommendations including one for proportional representation, only voted by a majority for a limited female suffrage. The restrictions on women's voting rights – including, by contrast with attitudes to male members of the forces, the withholding of the vote from members of the auxiliary services under the age of thirty – suggest little alteration in the treatment of women as second-class citizens. War had provided the opportunity for such change as occurred, but, it has been argued, was not the cause of it (**45, 55, 68**).

The First World War speeded, if it did not cause, the political advance of the British labour movement. The numbers affiliated to the Trades Union Congress grew from 2.2 million in 1913 to 4.5 million by 1918. The expansion of the engineering industries, where they were well established, strengthened the unions and made negotiation with them imperative. From the time of the Treasury Agreements onwards, trade unions were seen as necessary partners in the war effort. The unions' political wing, the Labour Party, was represented in the coalition governments from 1915, while the creation of a separate Ministry of Labour, along with promises of social reform, from 1916 were concessions to the new power of organised workers (Reid in **17, 45, 66, 68**).

At the end of the war, the Labour Party withdrew from the coalition government and fought the ensuing election independent of allies. Its 388 candidates (over 300 more than the party's previous highest total), secured 2.4 million votes (nearly five times the previous best performance) and sixty-three seats in Parliament. A significant number of second places in three-cornered contests, along with subsequent gains in local and by-elections, underlined the party's increased strength.

Labour were, no doubt, helped by the division between Asquithian and Coalition Liberals which had followed the establishment of Lloyd George's government in December 1916. This had a disastrous effect on the Liberal Party's organisation, resources and credibility. With Asquith openly declaring that he did not seek to defeat the coalition, his party secured a mere twenty-three seats in the new Parliament. Liberal disarray and Labour gain was compounded by the latter's recruitment of leading Liberal radicals or intellectuals, including Arthur Ponsonby, Charles Trevelyan, E. D. Morel, R. B. Haldane and Chiozza Money (**31, 45, 67, 68**). Labour's advance, however, reflected more than the chance consequence of Liberal disorganisation. The war had demonstrated the inadequacies of the traditional governing classes and, at central and local level, the contribution working-class leaders might make. It had drawn attention to social and economic inequality and injustice while politicians, backed by much of the press, had raised expectations without showing any signs of fulfilling them. Labour activists, in consequence, approached the post-war period with enormous optimism and enthusiasm (**31, 67, 68**). However, it would be wrong to overestimate the effect of the war on British political attitudes. Much of Labour's apparent advance could be ascribed to the increase in candidates and to the changed electorate. It is important to remember that the overwhelming victor in the election of 1918 was a Conservative Party intent on restoring, in large measure, the pre-war economic and social order, and that this party was, partly due to divisions within the left, to dominate government during the inter-war period (**48, 55, 66, 68**).

One aspect of the pre-war order which had undergone a severe challenge was the restricted contact between the state and the individual, characteristic of traditional liberalism. Increasing intervention in people's lives was not a process begun by war; the introduction of collectivist social policies had been very much a feature of the quarter century or so preceding the war (**43**). The demands of war, though, enhanced sharply the state's role in relation to the individual. This was seen at its most extreme in the case of munitions workers and adult males of an age suitable for military service. Voluntarism failed to supply either the numbers required for the forces or an effective distribution of the civilian workforce. Indeed, the war economy, by driving up wages in many sectors, positively hindered military recruitment. From 1915, the Ministry of Munitions had the power to declare any essential plant a 'controlled establishment' where 'dilution' of jobs could be introduced, strikes were banned, compulsory arbitration prevailed, fines could be levied for absenteeism, and leaving certificates severely restricted employees' rights to change their place of employment. Attempts to extend dilution to private engineering work were abandoned, along with the hated leaving certificates, in the face of widespread strikes in May 1917, but in the meantime the government had, by stages, moved to the conscription of adult males into the armed forces (**68**).

The increasing demands for men for the trenches led, in November 1915, to the so-called Derby Scheme, whereby men were required to attest that they would be prepared to serve in the forces if needed. The government gave an undertaking that single men would be called upon before married, and that military tribunals would decide on any claims for exemption from service by those called upon. This particular piece of moral blackmail, the last bid of Asquith's coalition to avoid conscription, failed. Only about 50 per cent of single men and some 40 per cent of married ones were prepared to attest. Conscription of single men followed in January 1915 and universal conscription in May of the same year (**33, 40, 45, 60, 68**) [**doc. 6**].

Conscription, incidentally, increased the proportion of recruits who were drawn from the middle classes, men in occupations not deemed crucial to the war effort. It did not, however, resolve the manpower shortage. The later war years saw regular reductions in the categories of men exempted from military service because of their civilian occupation, along with successive attempts to encourage National Service in vital industrial work. Nonetheless, the competing needs of the military and of war industries remained a contentious and unresolved political issue until the armistice (**40, 60**).

The government also intervened in respect of the supply and sale of food and drink, rather more readily in the case of the latter. By 1914, all areas had fixed hours for premises selling alcohol; in London these were 5.30 a.m. to 12.30 a.m., in most other towns they were 6 a.m. until 11 p.m. Under the August 1914 Liquor (Temporary Restriction) Order, the police and licensing authorities were able to restrict opening hours in order to maintain the peace or suppress drunkenness. By the end of 1914, over half the licensing authorities had acted, and closing time in London had been brought forward to 10 p.m. A government and employers' campaign against drinking was reinforced by the mid-1915 establishment of the Central Control Board (Liquor Traffic). The Board was able to restrict pub opening hours, in areas important to the war effort, to a limited period at lunchtime and in the evening. By the end of the war, only a few rural districts had escaped such controls. In addition, the Board fixed a 70 per cent proof maximum for spirits and also, in the face of a hop and grain shortage, took steps to weaken beer. There was a beneficial result. In 1914, England and Wales averaged 3,388 convictions a week for drunkenness, in 1918 just 449. The fact that the reduction was apparent among women as well as men suggests that the fall was not simply a consequence of the absence of young men on military service (**45, 57**) [**doc. 3**].

Governments were somewhat less willing to regulate food supplies, although steps were taken to maintain the availability and nutritional value (if not the taste and appearance) of bread. In fact, food shortages only became a serious issue from late 1916. In 1917 there were shortages of meat, sugar, tea, potatoes (until after a good harvest), butter and margarine. There were angry demonstrations demanding national food rationing, and walkouts where engineers downed tools to replace their womenfolk in the food queues. Even the Lloyd George government, misjudging public opinion, initially attempted to resolve problems by an appeal to voluntary effort. When this failed, more positive steps were taken. A bread subsidy was introduced from September 1917, reducing the price of a 4 lb loaf by 3d (1½p) to 9d (4p). The later part of the year saw also the establishment of Divisional Food Commissions and local food committees, some of which introduced local rationing schemes in advance of a national system. Thus Birmingham had ration cards for tea, sugar, butter and margarine before the end of 1917.

During 1918, the whole of Britain became subject to rationing of meat, sugar, butter, margarine and lard, while commodities like tea and jam were rationed in particular localities. A system which saw, by the end of the war, customers registered with retailers, retailers in turn with wholesalers, and 85 per cent of food bought or sold through government agencies, kept prices under control and eliminated shortages, queues and the popular discontent which accompanied them (**45, 68**).

A less obvious manifestation of government activity was in the regulation of the information which the population received and the attempts made to maintain morale and commitment. There was censorship of the press (tightened following the exaggerated accounts of British defeats and losses in the so-called 'Amiens Despatch' in *The Times* in August 1914) and, though less extensively, of cinema film (**45, 63, 68**). More positively, there were attempts to shape opinion or influence behaviour, co-ordinated from 1917 under the National War Aims Committee. There was a constant stream of posters on such issues as recruitment, contributing to war loans, the need for food economy or on German atrocities. The value of film was only realised in late 1915 but, following the very successful three-hour *Britain Prepared*, some 700 films were made for propaganda purposes, for the most part sober and factual in content and giving real insight into the nature of war. Public meetings were widely organised, especially in places like shipbuilding towns where morale was deemed to be low or doubtful (**56, 68**).

The government was helped in stirring up nationalist fervour for the war by certain sections of the popular press, notably that owned by Lord Northcliffe. One aspect of rampant nationalism was hostility to anything German or German-sounding. German names (including that of the royal family) were changed. Long-established London firms such as Ehrmann Brothers (wine merchants) or Oetzmann and Co. (furniture and china dealers) felt obliged to issue notices stressing their lack of any German connection. The First Sea Lord, Prince Louis of Battenberg, was forced to resign. The aftermath of the sinking of the *Lusitania* and of subsequent air raids saw rioting and looting of shops with German-sounding names in

London, Manchester and elsewhere. The government's response was first, in August 1914, the Aliens Registration Act and then, following the *Lusitania* riots, the internment of enemy aliens (**45, 51, 63, 77, 78**) [**doc. 4**].

The First World War, besides imposing itself on the lives and homes of a large section of the British population, had, then, been accompanied by a heightened nationalism, by a substantially enhanced role for the state and, after some initial hardships, by a general improvement in the earnings and wellbeing of many manual workers and their families. It had led, temporarily, to a closer and different relationship between the armed forces and the population at large. It had increased employment opportunities for women and had forced a new independence upon many of them. It had created a need for electoral reform and had contributed to the rise in the political power of the labour movement and the decline of liberalism and the Liberal Party. Some of the changes were significant and lasting; others failed to survive the coming of peace.

A continued acceptance of an enhanced role for the state might be seen in post-war housing subsidies and extensions in unemployment insurance (both discussed in Chapter 3), in the retention of rent controls, or in the continuation of a degree of railway regulation under the Railways Act (1921) or of tariff protection for industries such as chemicals, dyestuffs and scientific instruments, under the Safeguarding of Industries Act (1921). The spread of wages councils and, depending on judgements of the government's sincerity, the 1919 National Industrial Conference* could also be interpreted as acceptance of new responsibilities (**44, 45, 50**). The more obvious characteristic of the post-war period, however, was one of government rapidly divesting itself of its wartime responsibilities. Almost all controls and new ministries had been established only for the duration of hostilities. The case for an extended government function remained to be made, and the coming of peace brought irresistible demands from politicians, press, businessmen and even many trade unionists for a return to the old order. Disaffection among the troops, including the so-called 'soldiers' strikes' of 1919 against a misconceived and blatantly unfair scheme of release, forced the abandonment of an ordered demobilisation geared to economic needs. The slump of 1920–22 led to further state retreat (for example, from coal-mining and agriculture) and the collapse of many of the new wages councils (**26, 30, 39, 49, 58, 65, 76**).

Press, sectional interests and the slump similarly conspired to limit women's economic gains. The First World War was followed, in the short term, by no overall increase in women's employment. Indeed, the employment participation rate of women aged fourteen and over fell from 35.32 in 1911 to 33.31 in 1921 (**9**). In part, this was because women had become concentrated in industries which either shed labour or restored traditional male-dominated working arrangements once the war ended. Demobilisation was accompanied by a reassertion of men's economic interests over those of women on the part of trade unions, employment exchange officials and the press. Women who had 'won the war' or 'saved the nation' quickly became 'limpets' or 'bread-snatchers' if they sought to stay in work. The slump only served to aggravate women's employment position (**29**).

The war had brought some escape from domestic service and had accentuated the trend towards the use of women in offices and shops. Even in these areas, though, gains were limited. Many women were driven back into service as the slump made jobs scarce. The marriage bar was widely enforced in non-manual occupations. It was backed by a barrage of propaganda on the joys of motherhood and domesticity (**29, 32**). In the civil service, women were considered to lack 'flexibility'; male employees, even when the supply of ex-servicemen had been exhausted, were to be preferred (**132**). The Sex Disqualification (Removal) Act of 1919, which stated that neither sex nor marriage should debar anyone from holding any civil or judicial office, exercising any public function, or carrying out any civil profession or vocation, was interpreted negatively when tested in the courts. Married women were not, for example, disqualified from holding positions as a result of their status, but nor were they entitled to office (**12**). Thus, the aftermath of the First World War saw only a minimal expansion in the range of work open to women, the reassertion of traditional values and the continued use of women as a reserve of labour for use in low-paid jobs.

Women did maintain their political gains, though these, as we have seen, were limited in extent. Political representation remained (and remains) largely a male prerogative. The war did, though, contribute to a shift in the location of political power and influence. High taxation, the burden of death duties on a landowning class particularly affected by the high mortality among young officers, and the desire to benefit from high land values resulting from wartime agricultural prosperity, all contributed to the land sales of the early post-war period. As tenants purchased their farms, the landowning aristocracy's political domination of the countryside was diminished. Meantime, Lloyd George's use of businessmen such as Lord

Rhondda (the mine-owner) or Joseph Maclay (the Glasgow ship-owner) had, along with the outcome of the 1918 General Election, reinforced the business presence in government, and in a Conservative Party which, in the view of the aristocratic Lord Bentinck, was becoming 'thoroughly commercialised and vulgarised' (**45**).

The gains, and their limits, of political labour have already been discussed. Trade unions, though, had also advanced their political and economic bargaining positions as a result of the war. Their right of access to government, or to representation on committees or commissions continued to be acknowledged in the years which followed. Keith Middlemass sees this as representative of a growing corporatism in the management of the country's affairs, giving institutions (especially those representing the two sides of industry) a *de facto* share in the power of the state itself – defending 'democratic' institutions by 'unconstitutional' means (**18**). In the economic sphere, the needs of war had brought a rise in national bargaining along with a corresponding increase in the numbers and status of shop stewards at plant level. In spite of the difficulties which unions faced in the inter-war years, these gains, like the gains in earnings of their members, were, on the whole, defended.

Manual workers' experience in and after the war did, however, vary. By 1918, there had been a levelling out of differentials between the skilled and the unskilled and between wage rates in different parts of the country. After the war, the experience of those in the export industries was to compare poorly with that of workers producing goods for the home market. The contrasts within and between industries can be illustrated by reference to the building and coal-mining industries. On an index where 1913 = 100, the cost of living in 1920 stood at 265; skilled building wages stood at 250 and unskilled building wages at 328; skilled coal-mining wages were at 291 and unskilled at 325. By 1926, when the coal industry was suffering fierce competition in foreign markets, the cost of living index had fallen to 175, skilled building wages were at 182 and unskilled at 212, but skilled coal-mining wages stood at 170 and unskilled at 174. Differentials had narrowed within industries, but whereas those in building had sustained real wage increases between 1913 and 1926 (indeed, the post-war period had been kinder than the war to skilled builders), the miners had seen their wartime gains eaten away (**66**).

Thus the post-war world witnessed rather narrower income differentials within the manual working class, a process reinforced by the effect of higher than pre-war taxation on middle-class salary-earners.

Amongst manual workers, too, the war had accelerated the trend towards production-line work and de-skilling. The number of skilled and semi-skilled workers declined by 738,000 between 1922 and 1921, while the number of unskilled workers rose by 973,000. There had been no major shake-out of labour from the old staples nor, overall, any acceleration of the move into 'white-collar' work, but there had been a sharp increase in the proportion of women workers in this sector (from 29.8 per cent in 1911 to 37.6 per cent in 1921), with gains in shop and clerical work being particularly marked (7).

The state had, as we have seen, retreated – perhaps too far and too rapidly – but it remained more interventionist than in 1914. There were higher taxes; there were restrictions on public-house opening hours; there was direct economic intervention in forestry, brewing and the provision of housing; there was economic regulation in respect of selective tariffs and, indeed, the policies associated with the restoration of the Gold Standard, and there were extended social security responsibilities resulting from war casualties or the political decisions taken in respect of the unemployed at the time of demobilisation.

The Second World War

In the First World War, the state had extended its activities by stages and in a largely unplanned way. In the war of 1939–45, starting from a higher base level and with the benefit of past experience, governments sought, from the start, to extend their powers and responsibilities. Indeed, much of the legislation allowing this was already in place before war broke out.

One area of immediate, if not always effective, activity was in regard to censorship, propaganda and morale. A Ministry of Information was established to administer censorship of the media and to monitor and, if necessary, to shape civilian behaviour and morale. In addition, the War Office conducted censorship and morale surveys of the army and there was a postal and telegraph censorship employing, by May 1941, over 10,000 people (**95, 106**). Press censorship was, in theory, voluntary – although so-called Defence Notices indicated subjects on which advice from the censorship authority should be secured before publishing. The Service ministries and the Foreign Office sought to curtail publication of information – sometimes, as with the landing of the BEF in France in September 1939, with results damaging to government credibility. Officials of the Ministry of Information, by contrast, came in time to see the advantage of releasing accurate and detailed material (for example, on air raid casualties) as a way of curbing rumour and countering enemy claims and as a means of demonstrating the contrast between a democracy and Nazi dictatorship (**106, 122**).

As a final resort, it was open to the government to seize presses and close newspapers. In the case of the Communist *Daily Worker* this was done in January 1941 [**doc. 20**]; the paper did not reappear until August 1942. Other papers were threatened with the same fate. The Newspaper Publishers Association, and the *Daily Mirror* and *Sunday Pictorial* in particular, were put under great pressure during late 1940, when the government was sensitive to what it saw as attempts to undermine army discipline or good industrial relations. The attack on the *Daily Mirror* was resumed in March 1942 over the notorious Zec shipwrecked sailor cartoon* (interpreted, probably wrongly, by Cabinet members as an attack on profiteering), though on this occasion it was greeted by a political and public outcry on behalf of press freedom (**106, 122**).

On the outbreak of war, responsibility for the BBC passed from the Postmaster General to the Minister of Information. Broadcasts on a number of issues were only allowed with the permission of the Ministry. Individuals who held views considered hostile to the war effort were not allowed on the air. When the BBC extended this ban to entertainers and others who had supported the Communist-inspired People's Convention of January 1941, the resulting public debate caused such embarrassment to the government that ministers intervened to force a change of policy. Nonetheless, J. B. Priestley's 'Postscript' programme [**doc. 16**] was taken off when it became too political, as was the popular programme 'Anthems of the Allies' when Germany attacked the Soviet Union, since Churchill was not prepared to tolerate the broadcasting of the 'Internationale'. Overall, whether because of government pressure or because of the ideological and class links between the government and the Corporation's hierarchy, the BBC – as some, like Aneurin Bevan, pointed out – acted, with rare exceptions, as an uncritical mouthpiece for the authorities throughout the war (**89, 106, 122**).

Film censorship was nothing new. In the 1930s, it had extended to political issues, notably in the case of the banned documentary *Inside Nazi Germany*. From 1940, the Ministry of Information set up a special film censorship division, but the government's role, as in the previous war, was generally more positive. The cinema, in spite of a huge increase in seat prices – largely a consequence of the entertainments tax – was immensely popular. Weekly attendances rose from about 20 million in 1938 to between 25 and 30 million during the war years. Government intervention extended from simply faking newsreel material (for example, moving actresses into munitions plants to illustrate women's wartime activities), through the official documentaries of the Crown Film Unit, to the unacknowledged sponsorship of films such as *Millions Like Us*, designed to encourage women to enter war work (**89**).

In the early phase of the war, under Lord Reith, the Ministry of Information was very active in trying to influence public opinion in a positive way. Such activity stemmed from a basic misunderstanding of the popular mood, a tendency to confuse grumbling or critical comment with low morale and defeatism. As in the First World War, public notice-boards and householders' letterboxes were swamped with posters and circulated literature, including the June 1940 leaflet to every household 'If the Invader Comes'*. In addition, by early 1940, the Ministry was responsible for some 200 public meetings a week.

Much of this early activity proved counter-productive. Posters were frequently patronising or divisive. The 'Silent Column' series, aimed at stopping loose talk, coinciding as it did with Ministry-inspired prosecutions for defeatism, was seen as an assault on free speech; indeed the whole anti-rumour campaign was described by one of the Ministry's senior members, Harold Nicolson, as a 'ghastly failure' (**106**). Under Duff Cooper (1940–41) and Brendan Bracken (1941–45), the Ministry of Information (if not some of its fellow government departments) came to realise the distinction between complaints and low morale, but it continued to monitor public opinion. This was done using a variety of contributors including the managers of branches of W. H. Smith, of cinemas or of Citizens' Advice Bureaux. Use was also made of the BBC's Listener Research Unit and of two secret sources, police duty room reports and postal censorship. In addition, use was made of the rather suspect qualitative evidence on popular opinion collected by Mass-Observation*, and of quantitative assessments from the British Institute of Public Opinion. From July 1940, the Ministry instituted its own quantitative investigations through the Wartime Social Survey, the so-called 'Cooper's snoopers' (**106**). Findings were circulated to government departments through weekly and monthly reports (daily during the summer of 1940) and through special reports on particular issues. Though the methodology and conclusions of the reports were often suspect, they did act as a rather better barometer of public opinion than letters to *The Times* or *Daily Telegraph*, otherwise almost the only sources of outside views available to ministers or senior civil servants.

The role of government in censorship or in actively seeking to boost morale was bound to be contentious, especially given the democratic freedoms for which Britain was supposed to be fighting and the propaganda techniques associated with Dr Goebbels. By and large, attempts to meddle with public opinion proved ineffective and unnecessary and were, in time, substantially abandoned. Thus Orwell could write that 'the Government has done extraordinarily little to preserve morale; it has merely drawn on existing measures of goodwill' (**138**). This, however, misses the point. The Ministry of Information (if not other branches of government) had come to realise that this goodwill existed. Its officials recognised that the population would accept, even welcome, restrictions so long as they were seen as useful to the war effort and equitable in application [**doc. 19**]. Similarly, though there might be criticism of those in authority (for example, local government in towns affected by the blitz) or distrust of the political will to create a better post-war world, this did not lead to subversion. The mass of the population was bent on bringing the war to a successful conclusion. A government with evidence of this commitment was better equipped to take the steps necessary to achieve that end (**106**).

The treatment of enemy aliens proved to be another contentious area of government activity. Most of the 80,000 or so Germans and Austrians in this country in 1939 were refugees from Nazi oppression. When war broke out, Nazi sympathisers (along with a few left-wing refugees) were interned in a camp in Surrey. Other 'enemy aliens' were classified A to C, with the great majority being put in Category C and allowed to go free. However, in May 1940 the climate of opinion changed dramatically. There was fear of invasion and an obsession with the danger of a fifth column. The military demanded internment of 2,000 enemy aliens in coastal areas. An 'Intern the Lot' campaign was launched in the press. There were reports of employers sacking aliens and of their being turned out of council houses. Italy's entry into the war provoked attacks on Italian restaurants and ice-cream parlours in London. The government, responding to military demands, authorised the police to round up physically fit enemy aliens under seventy years of age, except key workers. The plan was to move them via transit camps, first to the Isle of Man and later to the Dominions. The intention was to give those 'arrested' time to put their affairs in order and to make the camps as unoppressive as possible (**89, 122**).

In practice, the exercise was a disaster: 26,000 Germans, Austrians and Italians were interned [**doc. 15**]. Many were given no chance to contact relatives; families were split up and poor record-keeping meant that many had no way of knowing the whereabouts of their kin. Their sense of isolation was compounded by the postal censorship which led to huge delays in the receipt of mail. In many cases Jewish refugees from Germany were placed in camps with Nazi sympathisers. The camps, administered by the War Office, were frequently a shambles. The Wharf Mills camp in Lancashire was rat-infested, with a broken glass roof, boards for beds, and only eighteen water taps and sixty buckets as toilets for 2,000 inmates. In spite of stated intentions, many sick or elderly found themselves interned, in some cases under canvas. A decision to impose a total news blackout, denying them newspapers, radios or books, added to the demoralisation of the inmates, who feared an invasion as much as, if not more than, the British. Gradually, as news of conditions leaked out, pressure for a modification of policy built up. It was strongly reinforced by the sinking of the *Arandora Star*, supposedly carrying dangerous aliens to Canada but with noted opponents of fascism among those lost.

By late July 1940 it had been agreed that administration of the camps should be passed to the Home Office. Investigations were launched into the selection procedure for the *Arandora Star* and into ways of ensuring the welfare of the internees. From August, releases began. The process was accelerated as the fear of invasion diminished, and by November 1941 under 3,700 enemy aliens remained interned in this country, although some 5,000 remained in custody in the Dominions. Given the reasons why many of the internees had come to Britain, the policy, and more particularly the practice, of general internment was especially unfortunate. Without doubt, it was one of the least savoury incidents in Britain's Second World War history, a history by and large free of the worst excesses of nationalist fervour associated with the conflict of 1914–18 (**89, 122**).

Perhaps the most obvious area of wartime state intervention was in relation to the labour force. There was no longer any question of the need for military conscription. A Military Training Act (May 1939) was replaced, in September, by a National Service Act allowing orders for service in the armed forces to be imposed on all men aged eighteen to forty-one. Subsequent Acts, under Churchill's Coalition government between 1940 and 1942, extended obligations for National Service until they covered, in principle, all men and women aged eighteen to sixty. Service in the armed forces was limited, in the case of men, to those under fifty-one and in practice, except for a few professionals (for example, doctors, dentists), to those aged forty or under. Difficulties in recruiting for the auxiliary services, especially the ATS, led in December 1941 to a decision that single women aged nineteen to thirty could be called up. In practice, only those in the nineteen to twenty-four age group were ever conscripted and even these were given a choice of occupation. From 1944, the needs of the munitions industries, especially aircraft manufacture, were given priority and all female conscripts were diverted into industry. (**113, 116**).

Second World War governments recognised the need to regulate the industrial workforce, but Chamberlain's National government. lacked the support of the labour movement necessary to implement effective controls. The Emergency Powers (Defence) Act (August 1939) specifically excluded any type of industrial conscription, while trade-union suspicions led to the emasculation of a Control of Engagement Act in September (**99, 122**). However, a Schedule of Reserved Occupations was introduced whereby men, above a determined age, in certain important jobs, were protected from call-up into the forces.

The Churchill coalition had an authority which the Chamberlain government had clearly lacked. Its Emergency Powers (Defence) Act gave the government almost limitless authority in pursuit of the war effort. The cornerstone of this authority, so far as mobilisation was concerned, was Regulation 58A which gave the Ministry of Labour and National Service sweeping powers. The Minister, Ernest Bevin, previously General Secretary of the Transport and General Workers' Union, always stressed the importance of voluntary mobilisation, but four major controls underpinned such activity: Registration for Employment Orders, Directions, Control of Engagement Orders and Essential Work Orders.

Registration for Employment Orders were of two types. Industrial Registration Orders covered workers from specific industries or with particular skills; during 1941 12,000 ex-shipyard workers and over 30,000 ex-coalminers were transferred back into these industries as a result of registration exercises. General Orders could require men over forty-one (the normal age of military service) and women over eighteen to give details of their current job or household circumstances. These were aimed at finding pools of unused labour, especially 'mobile' labour. Results were disappointing; in consequence the groups covered were slowly extended. By the end of

1942, women up to the age of forty-five, along with all men, had been required to register. The acute labour needs of the aircraft factories led, in April 1943, to the contentious decision to register women aged forty-six to fifty in the hope that they might meet local needs, thereby releasing younger mobile women for transfer elsewhere. Interestingly, between registration and their subsequent interview at the Employment Exchange, some 10,000 of these 'grandmothers' entered paid employment. This demonstrates the real purpose of Registration and of the other powers taken by the government: to encourage volunteers but to back this with the threat of coercion (**99, 116, 122**).

For those who did not volunteer, there was Direction. In all, there were some 1.5 million Directions issued. About half of these were in the construction industry, as a way of getting men to work in distant parts of the country on airfields, army camps or, in 1944–45, on units of the 'Mulberry' harbour* or on building work in London following the V1 and V2 attacks. From December 1943, Directions were the device by which National Servicemen were balloted into the pits – the so-called 'Bevin Boys'. The Ministry of Labour and National Service sought to limit the use of Directions – which were, of course, a clear breach of the voluntary principle and could obviously lead to a discontented workforce. However, Stammers calculates that they accounted for between one in seven and one in ten of all occupational transfers and increased sharply in incidence from 1942. If we add the undefinable number who, though not directed, moved to jobs unwillingly because they were aware of the government's ultimate power to coerce, we can assume that a substantial minority at least of the wartime workforce was subject to *de facto* coercion (**102, 113, 122**).

Control of Engagement Orders were designed to check unnecessary or undesirable movement of labour through 'poaching', using the promise of bonuses or high wages – a particular problem in relation to tool-room men in engineering. They came to cover virtually all workers in the engineering and construction industries. Advertising of posts was banned and workers were only to be taken on through an employment exchange or an approved trade union. Control of Engagement Orders were also used to restrict the movement of miners or agricultural workers out of those industries, and in a not wholly successful bid to stop women moving from more to less important jobs while the war lasted (**113**).

Essential Work Orders, introduced from March 1941, represented a further move to stabilise employment in important wartime industries and thereby to increase productivity. Such Orders eventually covered 8.75 million workers in a number of industries including engineering, shipbuilding, iron and steel, dock labour and coal-mining. Orders restricted the right of an individual to leave a job and made persistent unpunctuality or absenteeism (a serious problem in the shipyards or pits) a punishable offence. Employees covered by the Orders were compensated for their loss of liberty. Employers lost the right, except in cases of serious misconduct, to sack a worker. Dismissals, like applications to leave, had to involve the local National Service Officer. Orders allowed for a guaranteed weekly wage and satisfactory welfare and, where appropriate, training facilities for workers. On the docks, the Essential Work Order led to the beginnings of decasualisation under a National Dock Labour Corporation. However, the apparent inequity in the operation of the scheme (with employers being far more able than workers to breach regulations without being punished, and a far higher proportion of applications to leave being refused than applications to discharge) led to a critical TUC resolution in 1943. This and the derogatory views, expressed by employers and employed, on the effectiveness of National Service Officers, plus complaints about the quality of canteen and other welfare facilities, indicates that in operation the Essential Work Orders were not without their flaws (**102, 113, 122, 135, 136**).

One corollary of some workers being forced to move away from home to work was that they then had to be housed. Sometimes, for those sent to aircraft or government ordnance factories, this was in specially provided hostels, but often workers were billeted, like evacuees and many soldiers, on private households. The activities of the billeting officer, forcing war workers at 25s (£1.25) a week into already overcrowded homes, contributed to one of the more onerous of wartime experiences. Householders suffered extra housework, lack of privacy and rivals for scarce goods in the local stores or seats in the cinema; lodgers, too, lacked privacy, found entertaining difficult, had to suffer a change of diet and were frequently worse off than when living at home (**131, 136**).

The strain, in some reception districts, of meeting the demands placed on them was immense. In the case of Hereford, the influx of war workers (including those in transferred government departments) and soldiers led to a growth in population from 39,000 when war broke out to 51,000 in August 1940. In such circumstances, food and other essential supplies, transport services and the provision of accommodation came close to breakdown, demanding a co-ordinated response from different government ministries and voluntary agencies.

Attempts to evacuate children and, in the case of the very young, their mothers from bomb-threatened cities produced particular tensions. The children were stereotyped by the middle classes in reception areas and in sections of the national press as verminous bedwetters, their mothers as totally deficient in domestic skills. The middle classes, in their turn, were castigated for evading their billeting responsibilities. There is considerable evidence that government preference for voluntarism, the local influence wielded by many middle-class householders, and the derisory fines imposed by local magistrates on the few who were brought to court for refusing billeting orders, did lead to the poor and less well-off having to bear the brunt of billeting duty. Indeed, the lack of middle-class co-operation combined with accounts of the experiences of the first wave of evacuees (in late 1939) to restrict the scale and effectiveness of later evacuation schemes during the blitz and V1 and V2 scares (**91, 103**).

The blackout regulations, designed to avoid giving assistance to enemy bombers, impinged very heavily on most sections of the population. Accidents rose sharply, factory windows were painted over and artificial light used by day and night. Householders were faced with the nightly task of blacking out their homes. Though, in time, there were relaxations on street, shop and motor vehicle lighting, and the introduction of year-round British Summer Time made winter evenings a little lighter, the blackout remained one of the most burdensome of the day-to-day restrictions resulting from the war. Its replacement, by dim-out, in September 1944 was considered a great relief by many (**89**).

Blackout was necessary, although, for most of the people for most of the war, bombing was not an immediate experience. The effect of bombing on city-dwellers had been greatly feared. At its worst, in the blitz on London or, even more, provincial towns like Coventry or Plymouth, the effects were severe. Civil administration was, on occasion, overwhelmed. 'Trekking' – the nightly exodus to nearby towns or villages – was widespread. Contrary to media representation, there were public displays of hostility towards Churchill and a government that could let such things happen. Raids could instil terror into those sheltering or, at the very least, a weariness among those struggling to lead their lives amid re-routed buses, boarded-up or closed shops and the destruction of telephone wires or gas and water mains (**89, 109, 134**) [**docs. 17** and **18**]. But there was no

45

evidence of any increase in psychiatric disorders in areas affected by bombing, and the physical casualties were sustainable. Even bombing on the scale experienced by German cities did not lead to a breakdown of their social and political order or of their economic function, and although the suffering of some British cities was severe, it was nothing like that of their German counterparts.

People also had to learn to live with shortages and rationing. Shortages of labour, machinery, raw materials or shipping space led to a scarcity of many goods in everyday use. Civilian supplies of essential items of clothing or household goods were severely curtailed; those of luxuries like vacuum cleaners or sports goods ceased altogether [**doc. 21**]. Government trod a delicate path, seeking to maintain sufficient supplies of non-essentials like gramophone records to maintain morale; but, overall, the war years were a period of making do or mending.

Given the shortages, rationing proved generally popular. Ration books were ready from 1938 and opinion polls showed public support, but the National government, backed by the right-wing press, delayed implementation of any scheme until January 1940. Sugar, butter and bacon were the first goods to be rationed, followed by meat two months later. Cheese (at one ounce per person per week) was added in the summer of 1941, while eggs were subject to controls designed to ensure equitable distribution. The same summer saw the introduction of clothes rationing, using the points scheme. This had the advantage of giving the purchaser some choice as to how to use his or her allocation, and at the same time allowed the government to adjust the points required for different types of goods, depending on their availability. The points scheme was later extended to a wide range of foodstuffs including canned meat, fruit and vegetables, breakfast cereals, rice, dried fruit, biscuits and condensed milk. 1942 saw the final extensions of the rationing scheme to include soap, chocolate and sweets; the same year saw the abolition of the basic civilian petrol ration (**89**). Coal, due to the fierce hostility of the Conservatives in the Coalition, was never rationed. Nor, for rather better reasons, were potatoes or bread.

Rationing retained public support; indeed, there was some criticism that it did not go further [**doc. 19**]. It was seen as a fair means of distribution and as an indication of serious commitment, by governments, to the war effort. As late as 1944 the Wartime Social Survey* found only one person in seven opposed to rationing. Among women, who did the bulk of the shopping, nine out of ten were in favour. The figure was lower for men, especially in some northern areas where those in heavy industrial work had been used to eating more, and felt that they did not receive adequate compensation in the form of extra rations (**89**). The alternatives to rationing, given the great reductions in supplies of goods for civilian consumption [**doc. 21**], were the rapid price rises of the early part of the war (wholesale prices rose 50 per cent and clothes prices 75 per cent between the outbreak of war and the spring of 1940) or scarce goods selling out quickly or going 'under the counter', as happened with onions, rabbits and turkeys (**89**).

The government also moved to control prices, introducing food subsidies from as early as November 1939. From the time of the 1941 budget, there was a declared commitment to maintain prices at no more than 25 to 30 per cent above 1939 levels. Prices were regulated, too, on the so-called 'utility' goods introduced from 1942. Utility started with cloths and clothing and was extended, over time, to cover a wide range of essentials, including boots and shoes, household hardware, electrical appliances, pottery, furniture and bed linen. Utility goods were of government-approved quality and design at a price that the mass of the population could afford. Like rationing, utility goods were generally popular – which is more than can be said for the austerity regulations introduced for clothing in autumn 1942. The apparently petty restrictions on such things as the number of pleats in a garment, or of pockets, or the banning of turn-ups on men's trousers, did save, in total, a great quantity of cloth and other scarce materials. Nevertheless, the removal of the restrictions, in February 1944, was widely welcomed (**89**).

Subsidies were targeted on food (which had a 60 per cent weighting in the official cost-of-living index) as a means of holding down wage demands. They amounted in total to £250 million by 1945 but were, in fact, paid for by taxes on alcohol and tobacco which were lightly weighted in the index. A rent freeze on unfurnished property was a further means of curbing working-class expenditure and wage demands and, in turn, inflation. War Savings Campaigns and, more important, increased direct taxation were further means of combating demand-led inflation. Increased earnings and reductions in exemptions brought more people into the tax bracket, while the standard rate of income tax was increased, by April 1941, to 10s. (50p) in the pound. To ease the process of payment, 'pay as you earn' was introduced for some 12 million taxpayers from 1943 (**20, 89**).

Overall, the war did see a marked rise in real incomes of wage-earners. Wage rates rose by 50 per cent between 1939 and 1945 while the misleading official cost-of-living index only rose by one-third. A more useful estimate of wage-earners' living costs shows them rising by something over 50 per cent, but their weekly earnings, boosted by full employment, overtime and bonuses, rising 80 per cent. To this we should add, in many cases, the additional incomes of wives or daughters (**20**).

Experiences, however, varied and inequalities remained. Those in the engineering and munitions industries, and especially the aircraft industry, could, by working long hours, attain high earnings. By January 1943, the average in the metal, engineering and shipbuilding industries stood at £6 11s 6d (£6.57) a week and that of aircraft, motor vehicles and cycles at £7 8s 7d (£7.43). The average for all adult male manual workers was, by contrast, £5 13s 9d (£5.69) and for adult women £2 18s 6d (£2.92) (**92**, Summerfield in **121, 123**). Forces' pay – where, by 1943, a serviceman's wife with two children received £2 3s 0d (£2.15) a week – was even lower.

Nonetheless, there was a general levelling-up of manual workers' wages towards those of the artisan. In engineering, between 1939 and 1945, time rates for the unskilled rose from 75 per cent to 82 per cent of those for skilled workers; on the railways the gap narrowed from 61 per cent to 76 per cent. The weekly earnings of women manual workers rose from 47.1 per cent of those of males (October 1938) to 52.07 per cent by the end of the war (**89, 123**). To economic forces were added government policy, with Bevin using wartime conditions to boost the income of low-paid groups and to extend collective bargaining, notably in the cases of agricultural, retailing and catering workers (**87, 89**). This general rise in the real incomes and therefore living standards of the manual working class, and especially of the lowest-paid among them, was to accelerate trends towards lower maternal, infant and child mortality already apparent in pre-war years. By 1945, maternal mortality was 41.7 per cent below its 1939 level, while infant mortality had fallen by 9.9 per cent. Figures for female child mortality show a decline in excess of 70 per cent between 1940 and 1951. While developments in medicine and social policy, including ante- and post-natal care, played a part, the improvements in environment brought about by bigger incomes were at least equal in importance (Winter in **121**).

There were others whose incomes declined relatively and absolutely. The lower salariat, partly as a result of adopting the organisation and wage bargaining practices of manual workers, secured pay increases approximately equal to those of many manual workers. Salaried workers as a whole, however, suffered an after-tax fall in their real incomes of 21 per cent between 1938 and 1947;

after-tax incomes from property fell by 15 per cent in the same period (**20, 89**).

As indicated, women, like other low-paid groups, made relative gains. Perhaps the best rewards were to be found on the buses or railways where, by 1945, a woman could earn in excess of £4 a week. This, though, was still way below male earnings in those industries. Indeed, the railway companies' response to a demand for the 'rate for the job' for women clerks was to the effect that no other industry accepted equal pay so why should they. In the engineering industries, employers, as in the First World War, found means of avoiding paying the full adult male skilled rate to all but a handful of women. The government, besides continuing to pay its female employees up to 80 per cent of the corresponding male rate (and referring an equal-pay amendment to the 1944 Education Bill back to the Commons as a vote of confidence), only gave women in its training centres two-thirds the allowance granted to males. But equal pay had become an issue, as the appointment of the Royal Commission on Equal Pay (1944–46) demonstrated (**89, 92, 120, 123, 141**).

Women's representation in a number of major employment sectors increased dramatically. They made up 5 per cent of transport workers in 1939, 20 per cent by 1943. They comprised 17 per cent of local and central government workers in 1939, 46 per cent by 1943. In metal manufacturing and in engineering, where dilution was again introduced, proportions increased from 6 to 22 per cent and from 10 to 34 per cent. Such gains were reflected in women's trade-union membership which increased from 970,000 in 1939 to 1,870,000 by 1943. However, women's gains were often intended to be limited and temporary. The Civil Service marriage bar was suspended but not abolished. The Extended Employment of Women Agreement (1940), between the engineering employers and the Amalgamated Engineering Union, was only to last until the war ended. When the AEU, in defence of itself and its male members, finally accepted females in 1943, it was into a special category of membership with limited rights. Even part-time work, while popular [**doc. 29**], since it was only established for women employees, marked them out as a group with other priorities or responsibilities, who were not full members of the paid labour force. The Ministry of Health's reluctance to establish the nursery provision that would enable women with young children to take jobs was a further manifestation of the lack of commitment to women's employment rights (**92, 123**).

The routine, low-skill and repetitive tasks assigned to most women in wartime factory employment, the additional responsibilities which fell upon married women workers (shopping, cooking, washing, cleaning, child care) and conventional attitudes towards men's economic rights or reponsibilities, help explain why many, particularly younger women working full-time, did not seek or expect to continue in employment once the war was over. The Wartime Social Survey's sample of 2,600 women workers in autumn 1943 found 60 per cent committed or hoping to continue in employment (mostly single, older married, part-timers, members of the professions or those already in employment before the war) but 39 per cent accepting the principle of giving men priority in the job market. A British Institute of Public Opinion (BIPO) poll (January 1945) found 61 per cent of working women expecting to continue, including 81 per cent of those who had already been in employment when war broke out. Though the Mass-Observation survey of January 1944 found, by somewhat doubtful interpretation, a 'large majority' seeking to leave their jobs and settle down, those intending to do this were largely drawn from among the young marrieds. Moreover, there were sizeable minorities, 25 and 28 per cent respectively, who accepted that women should be allowed to continue in 'men's jobs' or that their future would depend on their economic circumstances. In short, the war had opened employment doors to women but it had not done so on equal terms with men. Furthermore, in order to enter paid work, women had needed to overcome considerable difficulties in their personal lives, as well as the obstacles resulting from the attitudes and policies of government, employers, organisations of employees and of themselves and their menfolk (**17**, Smith in **121**, **123**, **137**, **148**).

The Second World War was accompanied by an electoral truce between the major parties and (from 1940) by a coalition government. Following the defeat of Germany, the Labour and Liberal Parties withdrew from this coalition, and in the ensuing General Election Labour won 393 seats with 47.8 per cent of the popular vote, the Conservatives 213 (39.8 per cent) and the Liberals 12 (9.0 per cent). The result was stunning – namely, the establishment of a government committed to nationalisation and wide-ranging social reform. The *Manchester Guardian* spoke of 'a silent revolution', Hugh Dalton (Chancellor of the Exchequer in the new government) of 'walking with destiny'. The spontaneous singing of 'The Red Flag' at the first meeting of Parliament after the election could be taken as a symbol of contemporary exultation (**100**, **119**, **133**).

With hindsight, it is not difficult to explain Labour's victory. The success of independent socialist candidates and of fringe parties like Common Wealth in by-elections, along with the consistent lead held by Labour in BIPO polls from 1943, suggest a growing acceptance of the economic planning and collectivist social policies associated with parties of the left. The war did contribute to this. The war effort involved, as we have seen, a massive and widely supported exercise in government control and direction. The welfare policies, discussed and publicised if rarely implemented by the Coalition, were also very much a part of Labour's programme. The successes of the Red Army and the Soviet Union, acclaimed in the press and, if only to check the appeal of the British Communist Party, by government agencies, were popularly interpreted as a further justification of socialist planning.

Probably less significant, in spite of Conservative suspicions, was the influence of forces' discussion groups such as those organised by the Army Bureau of Current Affairs. The forces' vote, contained in separate boxes at constituency counts, was seen to be overwhelmingly Labour, but less than half the servicemen and women eligible to vote did so. If service life had a radicalising effect, it was perhaps less on the other ranks than on younger members of the officer class. More important was Labour's ability to win the support of an estimated 61 per cent of that 21 per cent of the electorate which was voting for the first time (**80, 95, 105, 114**, Pelling in **121**).

Churchill complained that war had disrupted Conservative organisation, by recruiting large numbers of the party's agents into the armed forces, while leaving Labour's organisation, based on trade-union activists, largely intact. In fact, the organisation of both the major parties had been disrupted by war. Labour's 50 per cent loss of individual membership (1939–41) had been only partially made good by the end of the war. The Conservatives, with more than three times as many full-time agents as Labour in the late 1930s, did lose far more to the forces, but such men were being released from October 1944 and the effect was, at most, to reduce the Tories' normal organisational advantage (**80, 105, 114**, Pelling in **121**).

Labour clearly did gain from participation in the coalition. Men like Bevin*, Attlee*, Morrison*, Dalton* and Cripps* (who rejoined the party early in 1945) were prominent, able and, in some cases, popular members of wartime governments. In particular, Bevin, as Minister of Labour and National Service, and Morrison, as Home Secretary, held offices which were very much in the public eye. By contrast, Churchill, in spite, of his popularity as a war leader, was not necessarily viewed as a desirable peacetime premier (a view that

51

could only have been reinforced by his style of electioneering in 1945) while, of other Conservatives, only Lord Woolton (Minister of Food and later Minister of Reconstruction) and perhaps Butler had a credibility in domestic policy to match that of their Labour rivals (**80, 105, 114, 115**).

There is little doubt, however, that Labour's greatest asset in 1945 had little to do with the war itself. The Conservatives had held or shared power for virtually the whole of the inter-war period. As such they were held responsible for the 'broken promises' of 1918 [**doc. 30**], for the unemployment of the 1920s and 1930s, and for the means test. Thus the Coalition Chancellor Kingsley Wood's cautious response to the Beveridge Report served to reinforce doubts as to the Conservatives' will to implement the social and economic planning of the war years. In addition, the Conservative-dominated National government had sought to appease the dictators and was clearly unready for war when it did come. The 'Guilty Men' of 1940 had mostly passed from the scene, but the Conservative Party was stuck with their legacy (**80, 89**).

The Labour victory was not quite as politically significant as it first seemed. The leadership did include men like Bevin and Morrison who had worked their way up through the organisations of the labour movement, but more typical were Attlee, Dalton and Cripps, members of that upper middle class which had predominated in Liberal and Conservative Cabinets since early in the century. Moreover, the Labour programme, the so-called 'Attlee consensus', was hardly one of doctrinaire socialism. It comprised a limited programme of nationalisation, mainly of public utilities, and a range of social policies, notably in the fields of health, housing and social security, agreed in principle, if not always in detail, by the other members of the wartime coalition government, and in accord with popular priorities as expressed in opinion polls [**doc. 27**]. Strongly influenced by the thinking of Keynes and Beveridge and by experience of government and planning, it was a policy to make a capitalist or mixed economy work more efficiently and equitably. As such, it satisfied the middle-class radicals and the majority of trade unionists in the Labour Party, but not the left-wing socialists prominent in the constituency parties. Much of it was acceptable, too, to the Tory reformers who were trying to change their party's image; in Quintin Hogg's words, to 'give the people social reform' lest 'they give you social revolution'. This group were in a minority among wartime Conservative MPs, but became much more influential after the defeat of 1945 (**80**).

The war of 1939–45 had brought not only an expansion of the government's regulatory role far in excess of anything experienced in the previous conflict; it had also, up to a point, been accompanied by the ideological conversion not apparent between 1914 and 1918. The adoption of Keynesian principles of economic management demonstrated a changed perception of what government could do. This was accompanied by a widely-held conviction, fostered by Labour [**doc. 30**], that many of the economic and social problems of the inter-war years had resulted from an over-hasty dismantling of controls at the end of the previous war. Tawney's classic article 'The Abolition of Economic Controls, 1918–21', the most cogent exposition of this position, actually stemmed from a government-sponsored research project (**65**). Experience, then, combined with the needs of economic reconstruction and social justice to produce commitment to a more positive government role in the post-war period. The election of a Labour ministry made this inevitable. The 1944 White Paper 'Employment Policy', committing government to the maintenance of high levels of employment, was one outcome of the new orthodoxy. The National Health Service, a new system of social insurance, and the largely uncontroversial programme of nationalisation, were further representatives of an extension in, and acceptance of, state collectivism which was to remain fundamentally unchallenged for over thirty years.

Transition to a peacetime economy was regulated by a wide range of controls over producers, distributors and consumers. Rationing of clothes, furniture, petrol, soap and many foodstuffs continued, as did hire-purchase restrictions, until the mid-1950s. Prices continued to be kept down by subsidies. Utility regulations and controls on building, investment and raw material allocations all continued until the Board of Trade 'bonfire' of 1948, many for much longer. Labour controls were the one exception to the general rule. For most servicemen and women, demobilisation was determined according to age and length of service. Learning from the unfortunate experience following the First World War, politicians and planners subordinated economic need to what was politically acceptable (**87, 88, 116**).

The demobilisation of the civilian labour force, by contrast, was intended to conform to economic need. In the autumn of 1945, however, in circumstances of acute labour shortage, the parliamentary opposition, the press, employers and even the TUC united to call for the rundown of civilian labour controls which were, in any case, being increasingly ignored. Even the Cabinet was divided. It was forced to abandon most labour regulation early in 1946. Contrary to intentions, something approaching a free market in labour came into being (**88, 115, 116**). Manpower budgeting, one of the great innovations of the war period, 'dwindled to little more than arithmetical wish-fulfilment' (**93**).

The period incorporating the Second World War saw a significant restructuring of the labour force, accelerating the long-term trend towards employment in bureaucracy and the service sector as a whole. The number of clerks rose by 937,000 between 1931 and 1951, by which time they made up 10.4 per cent of the workforce. Much of this increase was a consequence of the increase in central and local government activity originating in the war. Some of the wartime expansion in employment in engineering, metals and chemicals was also sustained after 1945: engineering employment stood at 899,000 in July 1939 and 1,240,000 in July 1947; metals at 765,000 and 910,000; chemicals at 238,000 and 330,000. By contrast, the decline in employment in textiles and mining, evident in the 1930s, was accentuated. Textile employment fell from 1,061,000 in July 1939 to 812,000 in July 1947; employment in mining and quarrying from 862,000 to 810,000 over the same period (**83**). In the case of these two industries, working conditions and past experience of unemployment deterred workers from returning to them at a time of abundant alternative job opportunities. The labour and skill shortages of the war and post-war years led, too, to a rationalisation and dramatic expansion of technical training, creating (in contrast to the war of 1914–18) a better-educated and more skilled workforce for the post-war period (**116**).

Post-war working conditions, industrial relations and wage levels also appeared to have benefited from wartime circumstances. Many of the welfare facilities established under the Essential Work Orders continued into the peace. So, in industries such as building, iron and steel, textiles and pottery, did the guaranteed working week. In addition, conditions of work in new government-provided factories set standards against which others – in particular, nineteenth-century textile mills – were to be measured (**116**).

The role of Labour in the wartime coalition, and of the prominent trade unionist Ernest Bevin as Minister of Labour and National Service, had secured a statutory negotiating role for unions in much of industry. This included participation, with employers, in Bevin's Joint Consultative Committee – which Middlemass sees as a further development of the process of corporate government. The continuation of Labour in office after the war ensured that the unions retained and built on the greater part of their wartime gains (**18**).

Wartime advances in the living standards of manual workers were also sustained. While the cost of living index rose from 100 to 184 (1938–50), that for wage earnings rose from 100 to 240. Much of this was, however, the result of overtime, piece-rate payments, and the regrading of workers. Actual wage rates lagged behind prices, particularly in the period after the war. Personal taxation remained, in the post-war period, at a higher level than in the 1930s, contributing to a reduction of income differentials (**1, 20**).

The end of the war was, again, accompanied by a sharp reduction in the female workforce. Forces' supply industries employing women were run down whilst, in engineering, the AEU saw to it that the provisions of the 1940 'Extended Employment of Women Agreement' were enforced to the letter (**92, 123**). Other women withdrew voluntarily to bear or rear children or to concentrate on household chores after their arduous dual role of wartime. The number of women in civilian employment fell from 6,718,000 in June 1945 to 5,943,000 in December 1946. However, the latter figure still represented an increase of over three-quarters of a million when compared to female employment in 1939. Gains were especially apparent in the chemical and metal industries, in central and local government, and in part-time employment. There were sharp falls, on the other hand, in the numbers working in clothing and textile manufacture. The greater numbers and proportion of women in the workforce, and the shift in their occupational distribution, were to be maintained in the ensuing years (**17, 116, 123**).

The increase was drawn from older age groups and from married women. At the peak of wartime mobilisation, in 1943, 42 per cent of women in paid occupations were in the age range thirty-five to fifty-nine; by 1947 the figure was 49 per cent. In 1931, just 16 per cent of 'working' women were married; by 1951, the figure was 43 per cent (**17, 143**). Given that it was decided not to re-enforce the marriage bar in the Civil Service (nor, by implication, elsewhere), it might appear that women had done rather well out of the war.

Against this, there is abundant evidence of women's continuing disadvantage in opportunity and status. Child care facilities, important to working women with families, declined. The number of day nurseries, the most suitable form of provision for employed mothers with young children, fell by some 700 by the end of 1947 (**118, 123**). Nor was there any substantial progress towards equal pay. War, as we have seen, had led to a slight narrowing of differentials and to equal pay becoming an issue. The Majority Report of the Royal Commission on Equal Pay (1946) supported continued inequality.

Women were held to be less reliable, efficient or adaptable. Lower pay was socially desirable as a stimulus to marriage and motherhood. Equality, besides being inflationary, would reduce women's employment prospects. Given employer hostility to equal pay, trade-union equivocation and a lack of leadership from the Labour government, the Royal Commission's view prevailed (**120, 123, 132, 141**).

Even concessions to women involved a reassertion of traditional views. The role of married women in the Civil Service remained 'a stormy question'. The decision taken was not to abandon the marriage bar but to retain married women for the time being. Bevin's motive, stated openly in Cabinet, was to keep married women in employment 'over the next two to three years'; the Civil Service was to set an example to other employers (**105**). In demobilisation, the decision to allow wives immediate release from the Forces, and the misguided attempt by Churchill to extend this to all servicewomen, reflected a similar traditionalism in attitude. Churchill's ostensible motive was to help meet civilian labour needs. His plan, however, and the actuality of women's demobilisation arrangements, involved treating women as a separate (and by implication expendable) part of the labour force, a group whose domestic obligations were of paramount importance. Provision of part-time work was a further manifestation of this view; one shared by many women. Evidence from the post-war survey 'Women in Industry' revealed that while only 7 per cent of women thought it wrong for women to go out to work and 24 per cent thought positively that women should do so, 64 per cent gave conditional answers. Looking after the home, a husband and, above all, young children, were seen as the principal obligations of the married woman (**116, 118, 123, 143**).

The post-1945 labour shortage ensured that working women were not subjected to the direct attacks of the period after the First World War. It also contributed to lasting changes in the range of jobs available and to opportunities for older and married women. On the other hand, there is little evidence that war had in any way undermined the belief that women were inferior and supplementary workers with prior commitments elsewhere (**17, 118, 123, 141**).

Women, then, remained disadvantaged, but within a context of more varied employment opportunity and, like men, greater job security than before the war. The population as a whole had been subjected to a greater degree of government regulation than during the war of 1914–18. Much of this had been, and continued to be, accepted and welcomed. Some of this, including excessive wartime media censorship or post-war attempts at labour controls, was widely criticised or rejected; other parts, including blackout and billeting, were accepted but not welcomed. Casualties had been lower than in the First World War but war's impact on civilians had been more direct. In addition, people lived with the memory, or popular accounts of, the previous war and its aftermath. The cumulative effect, as revealed in the many surveys and reports of popular attitudes at the end of the war, was a mood of war-weary watchfulness as people went about the often difficult task of building or re-building their peacetime civilian lives.

4 War and Social Policy

Social policy constitutes the conscious decisions and actions of government in relation to the social welfare of some or all of the people of the country. Motives can vary. Policy initiatives can result from a sense of social obligation deriving from awareness of unacceptable conditions or hardship; from a judgement of national economic, administrative or military need; from political motives or, commonly, from some combination of these influences. Social policy is often seen as encompassing state action on health, housing, education, social security, employment policy or the provision of personal social services. It also, however, incorporates attempts to influence demographic trends, gender role or (as in the case of licensing legislation) social behaviour. The twentieth century has seen an enormous extension in state social regulation. The timing of much of this suggests an association with war needs and circumstances. The purpose of this chapter is to investigate the nature and extent of any such relationship.

The Boer War

The Boer War demonstrates the contrasting influences of war on social policy and the difficulty of establishing any firm causal relationship. The immediate effect was to divert political attention, and potential economic resources, from two areas of activity, the provision of old-age pensions and of subsidised working-class housing, for which there had been mounting pressure in the 1890s. However, the rejection rate among would-be volunteers for the army (and the exaggeration of this problem by military men) did reinforce concern over demographic trends and over the condition of the mass of the population [**doc. 2**].

The 'condition of the nation' was already an issue. Statistical analyses and more impressionistic studies combined to produce a disturbing picture. Infant mortality, at a time when Britain's birth rate was falling more rapidly than that of rivals like Germany, remained (at around 150 per thousand) obstinately high. The increasing urbanisation of the population was seen as contributing to its physical and moral decay. Now, demographic trends and poor health were seen to be putting the empire at risk. Imperial needs legitimised government and voluntary action on welfare issues, most notably among leaders of the Liberal Party. In particular, it justified attention to the survival of babies and the wellbeing of young children, the next generation of adults and recruits.

Voluntary schemes to provide free or subsidised school meals for needy children existed before the war, as did the campaign to professionalise midwifery. The first health visitors had been appointed in the 1860s, and during the 1890s many of the new county councils had adopted and expanded the practice. In 1899 St Helens had established the first milk depot for mothers with bottle-fed babies. But the war does appear to have accelerated progress. The 1902 Midwives Act provided for the regulation and training of midwives, There was a substantial increase in the provision of school meals. The Report of the Select Inter-Departmental Committee on Physical Deterioration (1903–4), while denying any evidence of actual decline in the physical condition of the population, emphasised that there was much that could and should be done to improve that condition. The emphasis was on preventive action rather than on health care, with particular attention being paid to the need for an effective system of school medical inspection and for government-sponsored school meals. In addition there were recommendations on issues such as overcrowding, smoke pollution, distribution and handling of food and milk, work conditions, childcare instruction for mothers, girls' domestic education, adult drinking, juvenile smoking and state-encouraged physical training. Though the Conservative government failed to respond to the Report (except to appoint another committee to look into the issues of medical inspection and school meals), the subsequent Liberal regime did act on it, albeit at Labour's instigation in the case of school meals (**8, 12, 22, 32, 34**).

The First World War

The association of the First World War with the notions of 'broken promises' or 'the failure of social reform', whether justified or not, indicates that the war was accompanied by a concern with, or attention to, issues of social policy. The early twentieth century had already seen an increase in state collectivist activity, particularly under Liberal governments from 1906. Now war accentuated existing needs, concentrated attention on social welfare issues and created new circumstances which encouraged action.

In education, the pre-war Liberal President of the Board of Education, J. A. Pease, had announced his intention of bringing forward a major education bill in the autumn of 1914. The outbreak of war prevented this but, at the same time, emphasised the importance of the issues demanding attention – the physical condition of schoolchildren, the shortage of teachers and of secondary school places, early leaving and half-timing. Military and economic demands focused attention on the need to make the most of the physical and mental resources of the nation. The extent and efficiency of German schools, described by Lloyd George as the most formidable institution Britain had to fight, only served to underline the deficiencies of English education. Improved working-class incomes in wartime contributed to a continued increase in the demand for fee-paying secondary-school places. The numbers in such schools increased by some 9,000 in each of the years 1914–15 and 1915–16 and by 18,000 in 1916–17. Such was the demand that by 1919–20 these schools were forced, through lack of capacity, to exclude 10,000 would-be fee-payers and another 10,000 potential free-place students. Against this, male teachers were lost to the armed forces, some 200 schools were taken over for military purposes and increased numbers of children left school early, lured by the opportunities in munitions factories. Indeed, the 'abnormal' wartime employment of juveniles, along with evidence of increased child neglect and juvenile delinquency, contributed in no small way to public concern with matters relating to education and to the nation's youth (**3**, **25**, **53**, **61**) [**doc. 8**].

By 1917 all the major political parties, teachers' organisations, the Ministry of Reconstruction and the Board of Education were committed to educational reform. Lloyd George's appointment of the educationist and historian H. A. L. Fisher as President of the Board, and the War Cabinet's support of Fisher's costly proposals, indicate the priority accorded to action in this area. Fisher sought 'to repair the intellectual and physical wastage which had been caused by the war'. His 1917 and 1918 bills required local education authorities to submit proposals for comprehensive and progressive reform of their school provision. By introducing the principle of a minimum 50 per cent central government grant towards educational expenditure (an amendment to the original 1917 proposals) and by removing the 2d (approx. 1p) in the pound rate limit, imposed by the 1902 Act on expenditure on post-elementary education, he attempted to encourage a growth in the provision of secondary places. The abolition of half-timing, the curtailing of other part-time employment of those still at school, the introduction of a no-exemption leaving age of fourteen and the facility for local authorities to raise this to fifteen, were all attempts to improve the quantity and quality of schooling, and to combat the use of children as a source of cheap industrial labour. Concern for young people as 'citizens in training', and the need for a cheap alternative to a further extension of education, lay behind the proposal for day continuation classes for young employees aged fourteen to eighteen. The encouragement of nursery schools, physical education and recreational facilities, along with extensions in school medical services, were all responses to a heightened wartime stress on the physical condition of the population. Separate measures to raise teachers' salaries and to secure their pensions were designed to improve the quality of the teaching profession (**3, 25, 61**).

However, the measures Fisher did not attempt, and the opposition he met before the Education Act of 1918 was passed, demonstrate the limits to any war-induced changes in attitudes regarding education. The party truce, on which Lloyd George's coalition rested, meant that Fisher had to avoid any assault on the dual system of state and church in education, or any direct attack on the local authority administrative structure. Even so, local authority hostility to what were seen as 'Prussian' centralist tendencies in his original 1917 bill was the major reason for its withdrawal and re-drafting. Though some enlightened employers supported and introduced continuation schools or classes, there was opposition from the Federation of British Industries, along with organisations of employers and of employees in industries such as cotton or coal-mining where cheap child labour was widely used and was necessary to family economies. Lancashire, the main centre of half-timing, was also the centre of opposition to the ending of that form of schooling. Ultimately, Fisher had to compromise on continuation classes and, for an initial seven-year period, they were to be restricted to those aged fourteen to sixteen. Thus, government, media and public recognised the need for educational reform, and were prepared to pay for it. But traditional dislike of central direction, employers' attitudes, and the concern of some labour leaders for the family incomes of workers in low-waged industries served to restrict its extent (**3, 25, 59, 61**) [**doc. 12**].

As in the case of education, the war of 1914–18 drew attention to health-care needs while disrupting existing provision. By July 1915, a quarter of the medical profession had joined the forces. Recruitment continued at a slower pace, but by January 1918 the continuing demands of the military, where there was one doctor to 376 soldiers, had become incompatible with those of the rest of society where there was one GP to 3,004 civilians. The desperate shortage of medical personnel had led to the pooling of panel work* in places like Glasgow, Nottingham, Leicester and Birmingham and to the introduction of Indian, Chinese, Portuguese and Egyptian doctors in Cardiff, Liverpool and Burnley. Only the arrival in Europe of American forces and an unexpectedly early end to the war forestalled further collectivisation of general practice and the introduction of a scheme, agreed between the profession and the government, for the compulsory transfer of doctors (**72**).

Municipal and voluntary responses to infant mortality, and to the need to care for children if the physical condition of adults was to improve, had led to the introduction of Infant Welfare Centres and of Schools for Mothers. By 1914, there were some 400 such establishments. The war saw the number more than double to over 1,000 by 1918, including 290 receiving grants for teaching domestic subjects. From 1915, the Board of Education supported classes for mothers to prevent and treat infant illnesses while the Local Government Board gave financial incentives to local authorities to improve their midwifery, health visiting and other infant welfare services. 1917 saw a National Baby Week with royal and church patronage, involving central and local government and voluntary agencies in a concerted educational effort (**32, 34, 72**).

Incentives were reinforced by legislation and an extension of municipal responsibilities. The 1915 modification to the Notification of Births Act compelled registration within thirty-six hours of a child's birth, thus giving Medical Officers of Health information on which to act. A 1916 Act demanded more rigorous qualification standards of midwives, including six months' training, attendance at at least twenty births and a written examination. The 1918 Maternity and Child Welfare Act consolidated and extended many of the wartime infant welfare measures and incentives, requiring local authorities to attend to the health of expectant mothers and to that of children under five who were not in schools administered by the Board of Education (**72**).

The war stimulated action on infant welfare partly by its demands on manpower and its destructiveness in terms of human life. War needs and losses emphasised the waste in infant mortality or sickly children [**doc. 10**]. What *The Times* referred to as the 'growing cult of the child' was demonstrated by the Bishop of London during the 1917 National Baby Week when he observed: 'While nine soldiers died every hour in 1915, twelve babies died every hour, so it was more dangerous to be a baby than a soldier. The loss of life in this war has made every baby's life doubly precious' (**72**). At the same time, the enormous expansion of voluntary effort could be seen as an indication that working for the wellbeing of children proved a particularly satisfying form of war work, especially for middle-class women. Ante-natal and child welfare represented, in J. M. Winter's words, activities where 'collective virtue and national interest clearly coincided' (**72**).

The movement of large numbers of women, girls and boys into munitions led the Ministry of Munitions to set up a welfare section. The work of this section meant the appointment of sixty-seven welfare inspectors dealing with the welfare of women and boy workers and the placing of welfare supervisors in plant employing women or more than 100 boys. Firms were required to keep personal records of sickness and injury. There were financial incentives to establish or improve cloakrooms and washing accommodation and crèches, though here action was inhibited because the need for married women workers was set against the belief that women with young children should not be encouraged to seek employment. Finally, the quest for sobriety as well as for a physically efficient workforce led to the establishment of over 900 factory canteens feeding more than a million workers at a cost to the government of £3.5 million in lost revenues from Excess Profits Taxes (**45, 72**) [**doc. 11**].

Wartime consciousness of health issues gave impetus to the movement for the co-ordination, under a single ministry, of health services provided by the Board of Education, the Poor Law, the Insurance Commission, public health authorities and voluntary agencies. Before 1914, support for such a health ministry had been restricted to an informed few including the Webbs*, Morant*, Margaret Macmillan* or the medical men Newman and Newsholme. By 1916, however, Christopher Addison (a doctor by training, who was to become responsible for reconstruction), and the then President of the Local Government Board, Lord Rhondda, were pressing for the establishment of a Ministry of Health as a matter of urgency (**74**).

Though the principle was accepted, the advocates of the new ministry had to contend with the resistance of powerful vested interests. Approved societies* – the source of most government borrowing, and represented through the Insurance Commission – feared that the developing municipal involvement in maternal and infant welfare could lead to local authorities taking over payment of the 30s (£1.50) maternity benefit. The occasion of such payments, a substantial sum to working-class families, had been developed by the societies' collector-salesmen into an important opportunity for the sale of new policies. Even more troubling than the loss of this opportunity was the fear that a local authority takeover of payment of maternity grants could be the precursor of their handling all payments under the state insurance scheme, thus eliminating approved societies altogether. To add to the reformers' problems, the 1918 Maclean Report recommended the break-up of the Poor Law, with its functions distributed among the committees of the major local authorities. In a note appended to this report, Morant stressed the need for a Ministry of Health as a precursor to the redistribution of Poor Law services. The proposed ministry was now linked, in the eyes of the Poor Law Division of the Local Government Board and those of the thousands of locally-elected Poor Law Guardians and their supporters in local government, with the takeover of their traditional services (**8, 38, 42**)

The strength of the opposition and the unexpected ending of the war in November 1918 meant that the Ministry of Health was not established until after the armistice. Moreover, the Insurance Commission remained intact and autonomous within it; the functions of the Poor Law were not redistributed; and important areas of health provision, including the School Medical Service and the Factory Health Inspectorate, remained outside its control. Thus, while the war had stimulated the creation of the Ministry, established vested interests plus, perhaps, the return of peacetime political conditions, had managed to emasculate it (**8, 38, 42**).

On the day after the armistice, in a speech announcing the coming election, Lloyd George talked of the need for 'habitations fit for the heroes who have won the war' [**doc. 14**]. The use of housing as a political platform in 1918 has led to its becoming the area of social policy development most readily associated with the First World War. There was already a shortage of working-class housing before the war. It was an issue with both major parties, and the Conservative opposition had tabled an unsuccessful bill in 1911, calling for a £1 million Treasury grant to subsidise action. Shortage of materials and labour during the war meant that the building of houses, normally about 75,000 a year, came virtually to a halt. The war also brought rent controls, a response to rent strikes and unrest in 1915, while housebuilding costs were doubling and interest rates increasing by about one-third. Thus, the building of housing for the working classes became totally uneconomic. The need to house munitions workers also forced government departments, notably the Ministry of Munitions, into housebuilding, or led to government subsidies to local authorities or to private firms (for example, Vickers for housing at Crayford or Barrow). Such wartime activity not only established the principle and expectation of subsidy but also paid attention to housing design. The two best known schemes, those at Well Hall to serve workers at Woolwich Arsenal and at Gretna in Dumfries for those employed at a vast new explosives factory, both adopted high standards of accommodation and layout based on garden city* designs (**64**).

By 1917, in the face of evidence that the industrial unrest of May–June was, in some areas, linked to the housing shortage, the government was prepared to give a commitment to some form of support for post-war housing. Within the Ministry of Reconstruction, the Salisbury and Carmichael Committees drew up plans for securing sites, labour and building materials. The Tudor Walters Committee, established by the Local Government Board and reporting in the week of the armistice, laid down simple and economical, but improved, standards of design for working-class housing, including the provision of gardens and of bathrooms with hot and cold water (**38, 64**).

For all the planning, action on housing provision was to be a victim of Treasury caution and the delay in establishing a ministry. For as long as the war lasted, the Treasury refused to give local authorities the financial guarantees that would provoke them to action. The Local Government Board, responsible for local authorities until its replacement by a Ministry of Health, was unwilling to demand action. Addison, as Minister of Reconstruction, had no authority over local councils but assumed that he would become Minister of Health and secure that authority before any armistice. As in other spheres, the unexpectedly early finish to the war was to affect achievement in social policy (**24, 38, 42**).

With the armistice, fears of unemployment and of discontented demobilised troops made housebuilding a political priority. It would provide jobs as well as homes. Its importance, and the mood of the time, were reflected in the observation of Austen Chamberlain, the Conservative leader, during the debate on the Housing and Town Planning bill: 'We must push on with it immediately at whatever the cost to the state'. Though grants were to be available for slum clearance and rehousing, the measure was primarily aimed at adding 500,000 houses to the total stock over a period of three years. Local authorities were required to submit plans to meet need within their area. Having built the houses, they were to aim at setting rent levels that would be economic at anticipated post-war normal housebuilding costs (once the abnormal costs of the war and transition period had been reduced). Any deficiency of income in relation to the actual cost of the houses was to be made good through the product of a penny rate and a government subsidy (**64**).

The insistence on economic rents demonstrated the persistence of pre-war liberal economic principles, and ensured that only affluent 'heroes' would be able to afford Addison's houses. The oft-criticised absence of controls on the supply and price of materials was to contribute to a high Treasury subsidy to the houses and was to make the programme (and Addison himself) vulnerable to the anti-waste political campaign of 1921. But the absence of such controls was not through neglect by the Ministry of Reconstruction; rather it was a consequence of the delay in instituting the Act and the changed political and economic circumstances of the post-war period. Other under-achievements can be attributed to the attitudes of local authorities and to trade-union resistance to peacetime 'dilution' of the workforce. Against this, the Act established the basic principles of local government obligation and central government subsidy which were to underpin subsequent twentieth-century housing policy (**24, 38, 42, 64**).

The war affected government involvement in income maintenance in a number of ways. Casualties led to a marked increase in the payment of disability, widows' and orphans' benefits and to the establishment of a Ministry of Pensions in 1916. Inflation forced increases in the rates of benefits. Health insurance benefits rose by 50 per cent for men to 15s. (75p) a week and by 60 per cent for women to 12s. (60p), much less than the increase in the cost of living. The earnings limit for those covered was increased from £160 to £250 a year. Old-age pensions, after pressure from churches, friendly societies and trade unions, were raised by 2s. 6d (12p) a week as a temporary wartime measure and, when it appeared likely that pensions would become an important issue in working-class voting behaviour, by a further 2s. 6d (12p) to 10s. (50p) a week, with a slight easing of the qualificatory means test, in 1919. While this represented, by comparison with 1914, a 33 per cent reduction in the value of the pension, the £1 to which a couple were entitled compared quite well with the 15s. (75p) sickness benefit to which a family was entitled or the £1 unemployment benefit of a man with a dependent wife (**22, 38**).

Political expediency has been cited as the driving force behind the government's backing of the National Industrial Conference of 1919, for its commitment to the extension of the system of wages councils, which grew in number from twenty-one to fifty during the first half of 1919, and for its apparent interest in the establishment of a national minimum wage. This activity, like the appointment of the Sankey Commission to look into the future of the coal industry, has been seen (for example, by G. D. H. Cole) as a means of buying time during a period of post-war industrial unrest. In fact, while the political advantages of negotiation with, and concession to, organised labour were recognised, there does appear to have been a genuine, if temporary, commitment by Horne (Minister of Labour) and Lloyd George to this continuation of the positive role in industrial relations which had been developed by government during the war years (**30, 42, 44, 50**).

The biggest impact of the war, however, was to be on the system of unemployment insurance. It was anticipated that peace would lead to temporary unemployment as the forces were demobilised and as industry converted from war to peace production. As early as December 1915, the government decided that members of the forces should be eligible for a donation (seen as a form of paid-up insurance) to tide them over any post-war unemployment. In 1917, the Ministry of Reconstruction set up a Civil War Workers Committee to consider the arrangements that would be necessary to cope with civilian unemployment. Although the unpopular 1916 extension to the existing unemployment insurance scheme had added 1.1 million, mainly women and girls, to the numbers covered, the scheme still failed to cover some 10 million workers, 70 per cent of the civilian labour force. The Committee reported that the end of the war would affect employment in all industries and that no useful distinction could be made between those in war and other work. In spite of the hostility of much of the labour force to contributory insurance, convincingly demonstrated in the response to the 1916 Act, the only way to avoid chaos and improvisation (including doles) at the peace was through the early introduction of a comprehensive scheme of unemployment insurance. The government, however, failed to act and, as in other areas of policy, found that it had to move quickly as peace and demobilisation loomed (**38, 42**).

Addison, as Minister of Reconstruction, managed to defeat a Treasury move to limit the donation to 14s. (70p) a week, raising the 1914 level of benefit, 7s. (35p), in line with inflation [**doc. 13**]. Instead, bearing in mind the need to placate forces' opinion, the rate was fixed at 24s. (£1.20) for men and 20s. (£1) for women, with dependants' allowances of 6s. (30p) for the first child and 3s. (15p) for others. On 12 December 1918, days before the election, the men's and women's allowances were both raised by 5s. (25p), that for juveniles by rather less. The measure, carried out in haste and in a climate of political fear, established principles – payment without contributions, subsistence levels of benefit linked to individual, need – which were to shape unemployment relief throughout the inter-war years. In a continuing climate of political revolution abroad and industrial unrest and Labour political gains at home, with a mass resort to the Poor Law unacceptable to Guardians* and unemployed alike, the donation had to be continued until a universal or near-universal measure of unemployment insurance could be prepared. The Unemployment Insurance Act of 1920, like the donation before it, was prepared in an atmosphere of crisis and on the basis of inadequate actuarial knowledge. By the time it became operational, in November 1920, the economic slump of the early 1920s had begun and there were already an estimated 1.5 million unemployed. The needs of those who had not been able to establish a contributory entitlement, and the feared reaction of ex-servicemen faced with a 25 per cent reduction in income as they moved from donation to insurance benefit, led, during 1921, to increases in the rates and duration of benefit payments, to the introduction of 'extended benefit' or doles, and to the institution of dependants' allowances. To supporters of the insurance principle, this was the arrival of the age of largesse; to others it was a desirable step towards the acceptance of the right to work or maintenance (**38, 42**).

The positive effects on social policy of the First World War stemmed, then, from national need, political circumstances, and a change in the perception of the legitimate functions of government. National need was apparent in the move towards a Ministry of Health, in the attention to infant and maternal welfare, and in acknowledgement of the need to improve educational provision and opportunity. Political circumstances – including the war-induced increase in the influence of political labour and end-of-war fears of industrial and political disturbances – were prominent influences on measures to relieve the unemployed, on the decision to increase the level of old-age pensions, on the 'homes for heroes' campaign and, some would say, on the interest in the minimum wage and in extending the system of wages councils. An increased perception of the role of the state was already apparent in the Edwardian period, a situation not unconnected with the lessons of the Boer War, but the period 1914–18 saw increased state responsibilities in areas including pensions, the provision or subsidising of houses, regulation of industrial welfare, licensing hours and the pricing and rationing of foodstuffs.

It would be wrong, of course, to overstate the degree to which social attitudes had altered. Educational and housing provision were to prove early victims of changed economic and political priorities. Many local authorities were half-hearted or obstructive in their response to new obligations in housing, infant welfare or education. Attitudes towards married women working had altered little: hence the reluctance of the government to provide wartime day nurseries, and the post-war consensus of the press, much of organised labour and Employment Exchange officials that such women should withdraw from the labour market (**29**). But against this, there were more lasting effects of the war on social policy. Attention to maternal and infant welfare led to a long-term decline in infant mortality and improvement in the physical condition of the population. Addison's Housing and Town Planning Act did set a precedent for subsidies and improved quality in working-class dwellings; the 209,000 houses built under the scheme, while expensive, represented a fair achievement given the circumstances of 1919–21 and the measure's early abandonment. Finally, there were the effects on income maintenance, the establishment of a Ministry of Pensions and, above all, developments in the maintenance of the unemployed. The economic and political circumstances of demobilisation politicised this issue, forcing a generous response which it was hard to withdraw. For all the hardships of the unemployed during the inter-war years and whatever the petty meannesses of the household means test, Britain's unemployed remained better treated than the unemployed of other nations or most other groups of needy in Britain.

The Second World War

Discussion of the Second World War and social policy has tended to be dominated by the Beveridge Report, 'Social Insurance and Allied Services', of November 1942. In fact, in spite of its reference to the five interrelated giants of want, disease, ignorance, squalor and idleness which had to be attacked, the Report was almost entirely concerned with issues of social security, combating want. There were short sections on health services and the maintenance of employment, but scarcely a mention of education or housing. However, other areas of social reconstruction were debated, almost from the outset of war, in a host of reports, treatises and observations emanating from government departments, political parties, churches and other voluntary agencies or individuals. Nor were the ideas and policies necessarily new. Most of the principles and practices of proposed policies in education and housing were products of the 1920s and 1930s, if not earlier. Arguments for a nationalised hospital service, for extended coverage by the health insurance scheme, and for improved infant and child welfare services, had been in evidence throughout the inter-war period. Keynesian principles of economic management, on which an employment policy rested, had been gaining ground in the 1930s. Developments in income maintenance since 1908, though piecemeal, had been extensive, leading to a substantial erosion of the responsibilities of the Poor Law authorities.

Policy and planning in the Second World War were inevitably influenced by past experience. Exaggerated expectations of casualties from military action led to the establishment of the Emergency Hospital Service*. The particular fears regarding bombing were responsible for the evacuation schemes. The popular memory of 'broken promises', of being 'let down' following the previous war, and the awareness of the huge economic problems of reconstruction that would follow this, led civil servants and ministers to avoid rash promises. However such caution, as expressed in the government's reception of the Beveridge Report [**doc. 25**], only reinforced popular cynicism regarding governmental, and especially Conservative, post-war intentions.

The social policy schemes devised or implemented in and after the Second World War were, in the end, more comprehensive and effective than those associated with the war of 1914–18. In part, this was a consequence of the political strength of the labour movement during and after the war and of greater (if misplaced) confidence in the potentiality of governments and their planning. It was also, however, a reflection of the enormous scale of disruption to, and destruction of, previous welfare provision, and of the state's awareness of the need to make the most of what was likely to be a declining labour force. There was an enhanced respect for individual rights, but national need was at least as powerful a motive for action.

The immediate effect of war on education was disruptive. The plan, from 1 September 1939, to raise the school leaving age to sixteen for those few who would not be able to claim 'beneficial exemption' was abandoned. Evacuation, besides revealing the inadequacy of many all-age rural elementary schools, also scattered urban schoolchildren and, when they started drifting back into the cities, it was to find that school buildings had been taken over for different purposes (mostly civil defence) or that teachers had remained with their other pupils in the reception areas. At the beginning of 1940, only a quarter of children in London were in full-time education, while another quarter were receiving no education at all. Over time, in spite of the effects of bombing, something close to normal school provision was to be re-established, but higher education was severely curtailed, especially in the Humanities; no fit man was recruited into the arts faculties of universities after October 1943. War meant, also, the loss of teachers to the forces. By 1945, there were 26,000 teachers in the armed services and it was estimated that 26 per cent of teachers in the public education system were either beyond retirement age or were women who would give up the work once the European war ended (**89, 116**).

Education was a field of policy which, for much of the war, ranked below health services, employment and housing as a priority with the public at large. But it was an area which excited much attention and debate among informed groups across the political spectrum, including those with outlets to the media. Before the war, there had been criticism of unequal opportunities by geographical area or social class and, in the context of a collapsing birth rate, of the education system's failure to develop available talent to the nation's advantage. War, especially with Germany – given that country's traditions in scientific and technological education – only served to reinforce demands for change (Thom in **121, 130**).

Senior officials of the Board of Education recognised the demand for reform and set out to 'lead rather than follow'. In January 1941 the Deputy Secretary, R. S. Wood, observed that 'the war is moving more and more in the direction of Labour's ideas and ideals' and that, given their likely future political masters, only radical planning would maintain the Board's control of events. By June 1941 the Department's 'Green Book' (discussion document) was ready. The following month, R. A. Butler was appointed President of the Board. He was determined to press ahead with reform in spite of a veto by Churchill, who feared political divisions over the issues of denominational education and the public schools (**80, 98, 130**).

Butler sidestepped the issue of the public schools by appointing the Fleming Committee to consider their future relationship to the state system, not their abolition or integration. He won over the churches by concessions on the funding and management of their schools and by the introduction of compulsory religious education and corporate acts of worship. He gained the support of Churchill and the government by demonstrating – at a time when, following the Beveridge Report, the coalition was under pressure to reassure the public of its commitment to social reconstruction – that the initial costs of his reforms would be much less than those of the proposed developments in social security (**130**).

The outcome of the White Paper 'Educational Reform' and of the subsequent 1944 Education Act included greater powers for central government in a new Ministry of Education and increased duties (including the provision of nursery education and further education) for the reduced number of local education authorities. The pejorative term 'elementary' was to disappear, and education was to become a continuous process from primary, through secondary, to further education. In the public sector, secondary school fees, except in direct grant schools, were abolished. The school leaving age was to be raised to fifteen from 1 April 1945 (although this ruling was subsequently postponed for two years because the nation was still at war) and to sixteen as soon as possible thereafter. County colleges were to provide part-time education for school-leavers until the age of eighteen. Neither White Paper nor Act stipulated the organisation of secondary education, but a grammar/modern or grammar/modern/technical division fitted in with reorganisations already commenced pre-war, was in keeping with contemporary ideas on the ability to identify, by testing, different types of child, and was recommended in a Ministry circular following the 1944 Act. Indeed, local authorities were to find it difficult to gain Ministry approval for other forms of secondary reorganisation.

The Butler Education Act was more far-reaching than anything which could have been produced in 1939. It was intended to promise a better future and was widely perceived as doing so. But it would be wrong to overstress its radicalism or indeed its effects. Labour accepted the measure as the best that could be obtained in the circumstances. Conservatives, while in some instances regretting the limited and vague plans for technical education, welcomed the reassertion of religious values, the emphasis on variety of provision [**doc. 26**], and the protection of hierarchy and (by omission) of privilege. The proposals were a more of a step towards meritocracy in education than towards democracy. As such, they reinforced a trend already apparent, not least in the rapid expansion, before and during the war, of selection through objective testing (**3, 80, 82, 98,** Thom in **121**).

The principal recommendation of the Fleming Report, though little was to come of it, was that the independent schools should make up to 25 per cent of their places available to children from the state system. Privilege and exclusiveness were to continue and might even be subsidised from the public purse. Because the recommended arrangements for secondary schooling coincided so closely with patterns of reorganisation already underway before war broke out, educational reconstruction in many areas amounted to little more than a change in the name of schools. This, along with the system of selection for the different types of secondary schooling and the contrasts in curricula, facilities and staffing, ensured that the hope of 'parity of esteem' between the different schools would never be achieved. The raising of the school leaving age to sixteen was delayed until 1973. Nor did local authorities fulfil their duties regarding nursery education or county colleges; while in technical education, which had developed rapidly during the war, there was a lack of any coherent strategy.

Yet the 1944 Act did lead to change. The Ministry was able to use its powers at least to reduce regional inequalities in opportunity. The school leaving age was raised to fifteen in 1947, though not without a struggle within a Labour Cabinet faced with an acute labour shortage that the removal of a year's leavers (370,000 young people) and the consequent additional demand for 7,000 teachers would only exacerbate. The early release of 10,000 school and further education teachers from the forces, and one-year emergency training (providing 35,000 teachers by 1951), helped the education service make the adjustment from war to peace. Local authorities were required to implement reform of the school structure although, in some rural areas, all-age elementary schools lasted well into the 1950s. The educational opportunities of working-class children were increased even if there was little reduction in the advantages secured by children of the middle and upper classes. In the case of schools, at least, the major proposals did survive the acute economic difficulties of the late 1940s; in this there was a contrast with the experience of the 1920s (**3, 22, 81, 89, 116**).

There were many similarities between developments in health and those in education during and after the Second World War. The main contrast was the presence in the health services of a powerful professional pressure group, the British Medical Association (BMA). The condition of recruits and of evacuated children reinforced the evidence of nutritional and health deficiencies contained in surveys by Boyd Orr and others in the 1930s. Wartime shortages exacerbated problems, leading to the institution of a national food policy from the autumn of 1941. The difficulties of servicemen's wives or evacuated mothers in paying for GP care added to the pressure to extend the coverage of health insurance. The Emergency Medical Service was originally introduced to deal with anticipated military casualties, as was the National Blood Transfusion Service. War also disrupted services. Hospitals were bombed and one-third of doctors and dentists were called up into the forces; by the end of the war, one-tenth of those remaining were over seventy years of age (**22, 89**).

War, as before, drew attention to the needs of mothers, infants and schoolchildren. Local authority support of school meals for the needy dated from the Edwardian era. State subsidy of milk drinking began in the 1930s and had been extended in 1939. From 1940, the Ministry of Health administered a national milk scheme which allowed a pint of milk a day, at half price, for expectant and nursing mothers and children under five. The scheme, which was to last some thirty years, had a 95 per cent take-up by 1945. A parallel scheme providing fruit juices, cod liver oil and vitamins was rather less enthusiastically received. From July 1940, Treasury grants led to an enormous expansion in the numbers of schoolchildren receiving free or subsidised milk and meals. Between July 1940 and February 1945, the proportion taking milk at school rose from 50 per cent to 73 per cent. In the same period, the numbers taking meals rose from 130,000 to 1,650,000 (approximately 33 per cent) (**8, 22**).

The war years also witnessed an expansion, albeit uneven, in local authority infant, child and maternity services. Reception areas for evacuees came under particular pressure, and from late 1940 there was central government support for canteens for evacuated mothers, for emergency maternity homes and for residential nurseries for 'war orphans'. Bombing and the fear of epidemics were also responsible, in part, for the introduction of free vaccination against diphtheria (**22**).

Adult diets were enhanced through the introduction of over 2,000 'British Restaurants' serving 600,000 meals a day, provided by local authorities, and by a twelve-fold increase in the number of industrial canteens, from about 1,500 pre-war to 18,500 by 1944. Such canteens were either encouraged or enforced by the Ministry of Labour and National Service. Both canteens and restaurants had food allocated to them on an 'industrial scale', allowing extra quantities of meat, cheese, butter and sugar for those in heavy work. Adult welfare provision also included an increase in the number of doctors engaged in industrial work, from about 100 to over 1,000 (**89, 111**). It was, however, the Emergency Medical Service (EMS), instituted at the outbreak of war, which forced attention on the long-term organisation of health services. The government paid for and owned the beds, and directly employed the doctors and nurses of the EMS. The scheme, originally for servicemen but eventually covering twenty-six categories of patients, including blitz victims and war workers, incorporated the co-ordination of municipal and voluntary hospital provision and its expansion (by 52 per cent to 292,000 beds by September 1941). In October 1941, the Liberal Minister of Health, Ernest Brown, was able to tell the Lord President's Committee, 'we now have, for the first time in our history, a hospital service sufficient to meet the needs of the population as a whole'. In the same month, the Ministry of Health publicly committed the government to a post-war national hospital service. The EMS also made the voluntary hospitals, many of which had struggled for funds before the war, financially dependent on the government. The demonstration of what was possible and necessary in hospital provision, and the need to make some arrangement to sustain the voluntary hospitals once the war was over, led the Ministry of Health and the medical profession into planning post-war hospital and other medical services (**8, 22, 80,** Fox in **121**).

The BMA, the Medical Officers of Health and the Royal Colleges had established the Medical Planning Commission in 1940. Its Interim Report, in May 1942, accepted the principles of a national health service for all, the regional grouping of hospitals, health centres run by local authorities, and salaried GPs. The BMA referred the Report back, largely because of this last recommendation. Meantime, both the Ministry and the Beveridge Committee had been deliberating. The latter produced its report in November 1942, recommending a free and comprehensive health service. The Coalition government's White Paper, 'A National Health Service' (1944), reflected a compromise between the parties. Labour secured commitment to the introduction of local authority-run health centres with salaried medical staff. Conservatives maintained the independence and financial stability of the voluntary hospitals; they were to co-operate in public provision and to be paid for this. General practitioners were to continue to be paid on a capitation basis and to engage in private practice. All were agreed on regional hospital grouping and co-ordination and on universal, free, tax-funded treatment (**8, 22, 80**, Fox in **121**).

The main issues in the extensive negotiation, and latterly confrontation, between the professional bodies (especially the BMA) and governments, between 1944 and the institution of the National Health Service in July 1948, concerned the issues of local authority control of doctors or hospitals and the payment of salaries. In both instances the root issue was that of professional autonomy, though the prestige of the leading voluntary hospitals, by comparison with municipal, also shaped attitudes towards the management of the hospital service. The outcome was that the leading teaching hospitals did retain much of their autonomy, but other hospitals had their endowments redistributed and were placed under regional hospital boards representing voluntary institutions and local authorities. GP, dental and similar personal health-care services were co-ordinated through executive councils, half medical, half lay. Payment was through capitation fees, but doctors lost the right to sell practices or to set up where they wished. Local authorities had their traditional responsibilities – including those relating to vaccination and immunisation, maternity, infant and child care, health visiting or community nursing – expanded or made mandatory, but the controversial obligation to draw up plans for health centres was shelved, given the implications for funds and for building materials and labour (**8, 22, 80, 96**).

What had emerged was a tripartite structure of health services, administered by regional hospital boards, by executive councils and by local authorities, not the co-ordinated service that had been the ambition of early twentieth-century reformers like Morant or Newman. The universal and free service did enhance the health prospects of previously disadvantaged groups such as working-class wives. Cost, though, inhibited attempts at regional equalisation of services. It has been argued, notably by Fox and Thane, that the settlement of 1946–48 included little that the medical profession could not have accepted in 1939 and, by Fox, that Britain's National Health Service is not so different in principle from the health services established in other western countries (**22**, Fox in **121**). The implication is that Second World War experience was of little significance, that Richard Titmuss's emphasis on discontinuity is misplaced (**124**). It is true that there was an emerging consensus on health needs by the late 1930s, and that the main convergence of opinion during the war years was on the organisation of services. It is hard, however, to accept that without the war the restrictive powers of the approved societies would have been so quickly swept away; that the Treasury would have allowed the hospital service such an influx of funds and such growth; that the officials of the Ministry of Health would have become so convinced of the need to nationalise the voluntary hospitals; that Labour could have had as much influence on policy; or that the Conservatives would have been so ready to accept a free and universal, tax-funded system of health care. Similarly in the case of infant and child welfare, the early 1940s brought a sharp acceleration in the pace of change. War, surely, was the cause of this.

Housing symbolised the difference between promises and experience following the First World War. Surveys for the Ministry of Information and by the British Institute of Public Opinion revealed a great and growing popular anxiety concerning the availability of homes after the present war [**doc. 27**]. The situation was, indeed, dire. Building materials and that part of the building labour force not called up into the armed forces were required for construction work essential to the war effort. Housebuilding virtually ceased; the normal process of replacement and addition came to a halt. At the same time, half a million houses were rendered uninhabitable by bomb or rocket attack and a further quarter of a million were seriously damaged. In addition, wartime marriages and the rising birth rate of the later years of the war meant that there were hundreds of thousands of young couples with children seeking accommodation.

The Coalition, and its constituent parties, recognised the importance of the issue and of drastic action to resolve it [**doc. 28**]. The need for compulsory purchase to acquire building land at a reasonable price was recognised in the controversial Uthwatt Report on Compensation and Betterment. Though this report went too far for Conservatives, a compromise, allowing for compulsory purchase at 1939 prices in blitzed, slum or overspill areas, was incorporated in the 1944 Town and Country Planning Act. By March 1944, Churchill felt able to promise the building of 2–300,000 houses within two years of the ending of the war with Germany. These were to be supplemented by up to half-a-million 'prefabs' (in the event only 160,000, mainly due to a shortage of steel), their components largely built on the converted production lines of aircraft factories. The need to control the price of building materials and for rapid expansion of the building labour force was also recognised by politicians of all parties. It was the needs of this industry – where, due to wartime construction work, many had been called up relatively late and would therefore have a delayed release under the main demobilisation scheme (Class A) based on age and length of service – which forced the development of a supplementary scheme (Class B) allowing for the early release of essential workers. Building and civil engineering workers were to make up almost half the numbers demobbed in Class B where, apart from coal-miners, they were the only people eligible for block as opposed to individual release (**80, 81, 89, 116**).

All parties gave housebuilding prominence in their 1945 election manifestos, with the Labour and Liberal parties promising a separate Ministry of Housing. Public opinion polls revealed that homes were the key issue with the electorate and that Labour was the party most trusted to provide them. Ironically, the Labour government did not in the event establish a separate housing ministry, leaving the issue with Bevan at the Ministry of Health, and post-war housebuilding got off to a slow start. The slow release of local authority technical staff necessary for preparatory work, an inadequate building labour force, shortage of materials (especially timber) and household fitments, and Ministry rejection of what it considered unduly high tenders, meant that by the end of 1946 under 59,000 houses had been completed, compared to over 300,000 a year in the later 1930s (**115, 116**). The emphasis was on local authority provision (meeting social need rather than following market forces), with the 1946 Housing Act increasing the subsidy from the existing £8 5s.0d. (£8.25) for forty years to £22 for sixty years (75 per cent from central government, 25 per cent from local rates). Building licences and permits for the use of materials like timber were also used as a means of control. Indeed, public opinion held that 'red tape' was actually holding back housebuilding. In fact, performance compared well with that of the post-1918 period, and completions reached nearly 228,000 in 1948 before the effect was felt of cuts in government expenditure and timber imports forced by the economic crisis of 1947. There was also a strong commitment to repairs – a process begun in 1943, accelerated from 1944 in the wake of the attacks by V1s and V2s, and continued after the war – and to conversion of larger houses into smaller units. By 1948, the Labour government could claim to have rehoused over 800,000 families since the end of the war. Nonetheless, the squatters in ex-army camps remained and a 1951 survey suggested that the country was still in need of at least 750,000 additional homes (**8, 81, 94, 114**).

The war had, once again, forced attention on the housing issue. On this occasion, disruption of building had been reinforced by destruction through bombing which, though it may have speeded slum clearance, also damaged or destroyed many sound houses. There was no doubting public concern. The cross-party political response – increased powers of compulsory purchase, priority release of labour and the continuation into peacetime of controls on building or the use of materials – suggests that lessons had been learnt from the failures of 1919–21. On the other hand, the system of subsidy, inaugurated in the 1919 Act, continued to be the basis of action. The war of 1939–45 forced changes in the short term but, in spite of Beveridge's stress on housing as the key element in a person's standard of living and therefore health, had no lasting impact on the principles of housing policy.

By the end of the inter-war period, Britain had built up a wide range of income maintenance services and had begun the process of dismantling the Poor Law. The process, however, had been piece-meal, and there were wide, and arbitrary, distinctions between the benefits available to different sections of the population. The coming of war increased the demand on income maintenance services while the circumstances of wartime need, once reinforced by the make-up of Churchill's coalition government, ensured that this would not be met through the Poor Law. In 1940, the Unemployment Assistance Board – a national agency established in the 1930s to cater for those who had exhausted any right to insurance benefit – was re-named the Assistance Board and given a wider brief in the treatment of civilian distress. It paid about a million supplementary old-age or widows' pensions; the fact that three-quarters of these people had not been prepared to apply to local authorities for Poor Law out-relief can be taken as some indication of the extent of hidden poverty during the later thirties. Assistance Board Offices also dealt with other hardship cases including those resulting from bombing or evacuation. Since war, in time, almost eliminated unemployment, there was a dramatic change in the clientele of the Assistance Board. There was an equally important change in its mode of operation following the 1941 Determination of Needs Act. This, an inevitable consequence of Labour's participation in government, abolished the household means test, substituting an assumed level of contribution from members of a household who were not dependent on the person applying for assistance. These changes in the remit of the Assistance Board and in the method of assessing need were to be reflected in post-war policy (**8**).

By 1941 there was wide commitment to improved social security as a war objective. In May, the Conservative Foreign Secretary,

Anthony Eden, stated that 'social security must be the first object of our domestic policy after the war'. In August, the commitment was written into the Atlantic Charter*. Meanwhile, following an approach by a TUC deputation to the Minister of Health seeking reform of the health insurance scheme, the government had established an inter-departmental committee of officials to look into social insurance and allied services, paying particular attention to the inter-relationship of schemes. William Beveridge, who was proving something of a nuisance to Bevin at the Ministry of Labour and National Service, was appointed chair of what was intended to be an essentially technical investigation. Beveridge, however, set the committee a rather wider agenda; the government responded by downgrading its departmental representatives to the rank of advisers, thus distancing itself from any radical or potentially costly recommendations which might emerge (**13**, **80**).

Most of those giving evidence to the committee accepted that improved social security was necessary and possible. There were, though, differences as to the extent and type of change which was desirable, and some people, including representatives of the British Employers Federation and prominent Conservative ministers and advisers, questioned whether this was the time to be making firm, and possibly costly, plans [**docs. 23, 25**]. Beveridge, however, believed that it was necessary and even advantageous, in a democracy, to plan for radical social reconstruction in time of war [**doc. 24**]; 'a revolutionary moment in the world's history is a time for revolutions not for patching'. This 'revolution', however, was to build on past experience, notably insurance. It was to be no socialist revolution.

Beveridge proposed to consolidate the various insurance and state pension schemes, incorporating workmen's compensation and standardising benefit as far as was appropriate and possible. He sought to establish a range of benefits covering the major periods of need during the life of an individual and his or her dependants; the introduction of a system of tax-funded child allowances was to be the most important of the new benefits. He planned a system that was universal and compulsory. Eligibility was to be based on a flat-rate contribution for which, in return, the individual would receive flat-rate and subsistence-level benefits. The state, Beveridge argued, should encourage voluntary saving or insurance to build on this basic level of support. Above all, action to combat poverty had to be linked to action that would maintain health and employment and provide adequate housing and education. Indeed, the establishment of a free and comprehensive health service, of child allowances and of mechanisms to maintain high levels of employment, were assumptions within the Beveridge scheme.

The proposals for health and employment were, in fact, rather more radical than those for income maintenance. Universality was in harmony with the wartime mood and reflected policies in areas such as rationing or mobilisation. The flat rates of contribution and benefit reflect early-century Liberal thinking; the state may compel insurance to cover the necessities of life but has no right, beyond that, to dictate how people spend their money. Subsistence benefits were better than any which had existed before (and more than were to be achieved in the future) but they reflected a belief in the national minimum which, again, dated from the early years of the century and, when coupled with the proposed incentives to voluntary thrift, they demonstrate that Beveridge was no egalitarian. Only the tax-funded element of benefits (admittedly 56 per cent of the estimated first-year cost of implementing Beveridge's proposals) involved any redistribution of wealth. The contributions principle was based on Beveridge's view that people preferred insurance rights to 'discriminatory doles'. This assumption – which took no account of other possible options – reflected the view of the trade unions, and indicated a marked change of attitude on their part since the time of the 1911 and 1916 Acts (**8**, **13**, **22**, **117**).

The one area of his income maintenance proposals in which Beveridge was undeniably radical, though within the context of assuming women's unwaged role as housekeeper and child-rearer, was in his proposals for women's benefits. He proposed that single women should have equal insurance status to men. Married women not in paid employment should receive joint benefits with their husbands; that is, they should not be treated as dependants. Married women in paid work should have a choice of status but, if they contributed to the insurance scheme, they should pay less and get less, on the perhaps contentious grounds that men were more likely to be responsible for the basic major outgoings of the household. Beveridge sought specific benefits for women in the event of maternity, widowhood, husband's unemployment, separation or divorce (though the strength of opposition forced him to abandon this) and for domestic help in the event of illness. Few of these recommendations were to be accepted – an indication that in this area, at least, Beveridge was ahead of his time (**13**, **22**, **129**).

Beveridge responded to the government's distancing itself from his committee by systematically leaking details of proposals to be contained in his Report for more than six months before its official publication. He thus raised public expectation, putting the government in an acute dilemma. The price of implementing the plan frightened many Conservatives: the cost to the Treasury in its first year would be £302,000,000, three times its 1941 expenditure on similar services. Churchill was opposed to distracting the population from the primary task of fighting and winning the war; he was also unwilling to make bold promises that a post-war government might not be able to uphold. There was, moreover, the danger of alienating American opinion. Britain would continue to require American economic aid during the reconstruction period; this might not be forthcoming if the country was seen to be devoting resources to expensive programmes of social welfare (**22, 80**) [**doc. 25**].

The government dithered. Having decided that there was no alternative but to publish the Report, the initial policy was to get maximum publicity from it as a statement of Britain's war aims. Thus a popular shortened version was prepared, the Army Bureau of Current Affairs (ABCA) produced a summary for use with the Army's discussion groups, the BBC broadcast details in twenty-two different languages. Press and public, at a time when military events were demonstrating that the allies were getting the upper hand in the war, gave the Report an almost hysterical welcome. Then the government abruptly changed tack. The ABCA summary was withdrawn and subsequently, with some embarrassment, reissued in revised form. An official silence covered manoeuvres and wrangling among the parties of the Coalition. Eventually, ministers agreed to plan, but not – except in the case of child allowances – to legislate. The government's commitment, as expressed in the parliamentary debate on the Beveridge Report in February 1943, did not go far enough, and 121 Members of Parliament, including all but two Labour backbenchers, voted for a critical amendment. In the following month, Churchill, belatedly recognising the popular consensus, was to promise, as part of an admittedly rather vague four-year plan of reconstruction, 'national compulsory insurance for all classes for all purposes from the cradle to the grave'. But he was too late. Opinion polls continued to show popular suspicion of government and especially Conservative intentions. Labour ministers had pushed the government further than its Conservative members had wanted to go; Labour backbenchers had demonstrated that they would have gone further. From this point on, Labour, of the two major parties, was the one seen as committed to implementing Beveridge's proposals (**80, 89**).

The Coalition government's attention to the issue of social

security led to the White Paper 'Social Insurance' of September 1944, to the establishment of a Ministry of National Insurance in November 1944, and to legislation during the spring of 1945 providing for family (that is, child) allowances. The White Paper proposed, like Beveridge, a comprehensive and universal coverage, justifying this by analogy with 'the solidarity and unity of the nation which in war have been its bulwark against aggression'. It stressed the primary need to pursue the economic growth which would minimise poverty, but accepted that there would remain the need to protect people against the 'hazards of personal misfortune over which individuals have little or no control'. Subsistence benefits, however, were rejected as impracticable. Falling money values, contrasting regional rent levels, and price increases which varied by commodity or place, meant that a universal flat-rate subsistence benefit could not be provided except at a level demanding contributions beyond the means of large sections of the workforce. The principle of varying payments according to need was dismissed since it was not insurance.

Family allowances, paid from August 1946, gave the employed the dependants' benefit allowed the unemployed since the legislative adjustments following the First World War. They were universal (that is, not means-tested) and were paid for the second and subsequent children; the exclusion of the first child had been accepted by Beveridge as an economy measure. The rate fixed, of 5s. (25p) a child, was below the 8s. (40p) recommended by Beveridge; this was justified on the grounds of other non-monetary benefits, including subsidised milk or school meals, now provided by the state. Given the concern to promote population growth, the level of benefit had to be adequate. Agitation for child allowances dated back to Edwardian demands for the endowment of motherhood. The war had, though, speeded their introduction. Trade-union fears that such allowances would be used to justify continued low wages had been reduced, as had the Treasury's power to obstruct the measure. War had drawn attention, once again, to the importance of a healthy and numerous population. The state, by introducing family allowances, accepted, in principle, a degree of responsibility for the raising of every family with two or more children (**8, 13, 22, 107**).

The income maintenance policies of the post-war Labour government were basically those of the Coalition. The National Insurance (Industrial Injuries) Act (1946) gave workers compensation without the need to resort to the courts; it also pooled the risks between different industries. Benefit, like that for wartime military casualties, was higher than normal insurance benefits. Separate provision and higher rates were illogical and had been opposed by Beveridge. Society and the state, however, deemed such casualties worthy of favoured treatment in comparison with the rest of the population.

The National Insurance Act (1946) accepted the principle of universality and attempted a subsistence level of benefit. Flat-rate contributions and benefits were adopted but differed according to classification (employed, self-employed, non-employed), age and sex. The standard sickness, unemployment and retirement benefit was fixed at 26s. (£1.30), representing a 2s. (10p) increase on unemployment benefit levels, an 8s. (40p) increase on sickness benefit and a 16s. (80p) increase on pensions. There were also allowances of 16s. (80p) for a wife and 7s. 6d (37p) for the first child. They were paid in full from October 1946; Beveridge had recommended, on grounds of cost, a twenty-year timescale for bringing retirement pensions up to the full amount. There was no place in the system for the approved societies. Beveridge had been hostile to them because of the unequal sickness benefits they had provided. He had proposed nationalising the profit-making industrial assurance societies and using approved societies to distribute benefits as a means of encouraging additional voluntary insurance. The government did neither (**8, 13**).

The National Assistance Act (1948) completed post-war social security provision. It formally abolished the Poor Law, transferring financial relief for the needy from the locality (rate-funded) to a central authority (tax-funded). It was intended to provide a supplementary source of relief for those who, for one reason or another, could not claim adequate benefit under National Insurance. The National Assistance Board evolved from the Assistance Board; like its predecessor it used a personal rather than household means test, disregarding some capital and income in assessing entitlement. National Assistance was intended as a last resort for the few. In fact, because insured benefits had been fixed at a bare subsistence, if that, and because of inflation and changing perceptions of what constituted an acceptable minimum, National Assistance and its successor benefits were to become major providers in the decades which followed the war (**8, 13**).

To what extent did social security change between 1939 and 1948, and how far was this due to the war? There was a new consensus on national responsibility, on the need for a universal and comprehensive system. Inequities had been reduced and there was an attempt to provide a subsistence level of benefit. The Poor Law and its principles were, in intent at least, rejected. The war had established belief in social solidarity and a commitment to social security as a war aim. The nation's ability to meet the prodigious costs of war, albeit with American aid, had undermined the argument that Britain could not afford a comprehensive system of social insurance. The war had forced action on behalf of pensioners and other needy groups; old systems had proved inadequate and something had to be provided to replace them. War had weakened the opponents of a greatly enhanced social security system – the Treasury and the Chamberlainites – and had greatly strengthened those, notably Labour and the unions, who supported such advance. On the other hand, we should not disregard the extent to which income maintenance provision had developed during the inter-war years, particularly with regard to national responsibility. Nor should we forget the ongoing view of many, but not all, employers, or of the bulk of Conservative MPs, that there would be other, more pressing, commitments during the reconstruction period. That said, the debate, by 1943, was about what *could* be done rather than what *should* be done. That, in itself, represented a marked and war-induced contrast with the attitudes of the 1930s.

The White Paper 'Employment Policy', published in June 1944, committed governments to 'the maintenance of a high and stable level of employment after the war' – on the face of it, a dramatic contrast to the policies of the 1930s. War had brought many academic economists, not least Keynes, into government service. It brought a commitment to planning and to economic regulation and, with this, a greatly enhanced confidence in the power of governments [**doc. 22**] to manage the economy. Survey evidence suggested that fear of post-war unemployment could become a major political issue. The prominence that Beveridge gave, in 'Social Insurance and Allied Services', to maintaining employment, and the fact that he subsequently embarked on a private survey of ways to achieve this, made the issue of employment a government priority. It did not, however, eliminate divisions, principally between the Treasury and the Economic Section of the Cabinet Office, the latter a creation of the war, as to the measures that should be undertaken.

Though the objective of the White Paper was bold, the methods it proposed represented a compromise between the opposing economic factions within government. There was no clear-cut commitment to the use of fiscal devices of demand management or to deficit budgeting. The main means of combating cyclical unemployment was to be local authority investment in infrastructure.

Otherwise, the emphasis was on a more mobile workforce and a more dynamic regional policy. Beveridge's own report, 'Full Employment in a Free Society', published six months later, was much more radical both in the means proposed – including the use of taxation, government borrowing and deficit budgeting to manipulate public and private investment and consumer demand – and in its target of an unemployment level of not more than 3 per cent (**10**, **20**, **88**, Macleod in **121**).

Government had clearly taken on new commitments; moreover, the war was followed by a quarter of a century of almost unbroken 'full employment'. Did this represent a Keynesian revolution in economic policy? The White Paper measures for combating cyclical unemployment amounted to little more than the recommendations of the 1909 Minority Report of the Royal Commission on the Poor Laws. The economist R. C. O. Matthews, writing in 1968, convincingly demonstrated that the maintenance of high employment in the 1950s and 1960s was the result of higher investment and higher exports. Governments did not use the device of the budget deficit: indeed they operated with persistent budget surpluses. More recently, J. D. Tomlinson has argued that, though there were great changes in government economic roles between the 1930s and the 1950s, most notably in the attempts at fine-tuning demand management, these were a consequence of institutional factors (including the evolution of a national accountancy system and the vast growth in public expenditure), not of a new economic orthodoxy. Most important, for Tomlinson, the key element of a Keynesian revolution – subordinating fiscal policy to the needs of employment – was never achieved in Britain (**110**, **125**, **126**).

This, though, is unduly negative. The 'unconvincing' White Paper and the divisions between economists in wartime government service certainly undermine any assumptions of monolithic Keynesian orthodoxy by the mid-forties. But Matthews saw the increased investment in the 1950s as a consequence of changed entrepreneurial attitudes resulting from a confidence that governments could and would manage the economy in order to avoid slumps and unemployment (**110**, Macleod in **121**). Nor should deficit budgeting be seen as peculiar to, or the essence of, Keynesianism. A budget deficit had been used in 1919 to avert unemployment; Keynesianism included not only the use of the budget as economic regulator but also a 'close economic monitoring of the economy and its principal aggregates, and the integration of this activity into monetary and fiscal policy-making' (**84**, **85**).

Governments' role in the maintenance of employment during the post-war years may, with hindsight, appear to have been minimal. Nonetheless, the objective of keeping people in work was, for over thirty years, accepted as a primary function and governments thought they had the Keynesian tools to achieve this.

Positive changes in social policy can, then, be seen, as in the case of those of the First World War, to result from national need, the political circumstances created by the war, and war-induced changes in the perception of government functions and capabilities. National need was the driving force behind developments in technical education and the establishment of the Emergency Medical Service leading to the nationalisation of hospitals. It lay behind policy developments aiding the nutrition of mothers, infants and schoolchildren. It led to extensions in the activities of the Assistance Board, further undermining the role of the Poor Law. It focused attention on the housing question.

Political circumstances aiding extensions in social policy included the incorporation of Labour in the Coalition (and the not unconnected Labour victory in the 1945 election), the discrediting of the Chamberlainite regime of the thirties, and the re-emergence of Churchill who, like the Labour leaders, was keen to reduce Treasury influence on policy. The government's extensive monitoring of public opinion increased the pressures for action; ministers were conscious, perhaps over-conscious, of the popular mood of being let down 'last time' and of concern regarding jobs and housing. Early initiatives by Board of Education officials or the medical profession, determined to shape any change which did occur, plus the activities and public profile of Beveridge, were a further stimulus to action. The shape of this action, in particular the drive to universal and comprehensive provision, was a product of wartime experiences and assumptions. In terms of government role, it might be argued that the war of 1939–45 did not involve such a break with precedent as that of 1914–18. On the other hand, there was rather more planning and less of a piecemeal build-up of involvement. In particular, there were significant developments in economic management. This, as we have seen, made possible the commitment to an employment policy. It also underpinned the arguments of those demanding expensive programmes in health or social security; if the country could organise its economic affairs to fight a war on this scale successfully, then it could surely organise its resources to achieve peacetime welfare objectives.

There were, of course, counter-influences. Coalition divisions

87

delayed action in most areas of social security and restricted the extent of change in education. Churchill's concern not to divert the population from the war effort or to promise what might not be practicable were further obstacles. So, too, was the fear of the reaction of Britain's American bankers to over-ambitious welfare schemes. The justification for this fear was demonstrated in the economic difficulties of the immediate post-war years. Scarce resources and the austerity measures of the late 1940s hindered educational and housing provision and prevented the establishment of adequate levels of social insurance benefit.

Many of the ideas of the war and post-war period were little changed from those of earlier in the century. We have seen that social reforms in education, health care, income maintenance and even employment policy drew heavily on earlier ideas or, in some cases, on earlier practices. Housing subsidies were clearly the linear descendant of the Addison Act and its successors. Attitudes to women showed a similar continuity. Though Beveridge recognised the economic value of the domestic function, and though he sought better treatment of female workers, he still assumed the primacy of women's child-rearing and household role. This attitude was apparent, too, in the Report of the Royal Commission on Equal Pay and in the post-war closure of the day nurseries which had enabled married women with children to engage in paid work. Family allowances, which were meant to encourage childbirth and population growth, were another incentive to married women to choose domesticity.

Overall, though, the Second World War does appear to have been accompanied by a change in social policy. The opposition to comprehensive and universal non-stigmatising policies in education, health and income maintenance had been defeated. There was an attempt at a new level of provision: optimum health and education services, subsistence levels of social security. While many of the high hopes of the immediate post-war years were later frustrated, governments in the 1940s and 1950s did not disengage themselves from their social or economic commitments. This was an important, even if not the only, contribution to greater security for the population as a whole.

Part Three: Assessment

There can be little argument that British society, in the period after 1945, differed significantly from that of 1914 or even from that of 1939. There was greater security of employment and less material poverty. The population, taken as a whole, was healthier and better housed. There were also greater educational opportunities. Universalist and comprehensive social policies had replaced the selective, restricted and often stigmatising provision of the Edwardian era. Though blatant inequalities remained, trends in earnings and in taxation had, along with state-provided benefits in cash and kind, reduced differences in real incomes. Women had gained in political and economic status. Organised labour, in the form of trade unions and the Labour Party, had become a major force. Were wars the cause of these developments and, if so, how?

War had contributed to both guided and unguided social change. Perceived political needs had influenced the introduction of a state subsidy for housing and a subsistence-level dole at the end of the First World War which had shaped subsequent developments in housing and income maintenance policy respectively. Political forces had dictated, too, the widespread welfare planning of the period 1942–44; activity which served to heighten the popular expectations to which it was, initially, a response.

National military or economic need drew attention to the importance of making the most of the present and future labour resources available to the country and to deficiencies in existing health and educational provision. Policies aimed at the care of mothers and infants (evident in or after the wars of 1899–1902, 1914–18 and 1939–45) were, in part, a response to this awareness; so was the establishment, however disappointing in practice, of a Ministry of Health in 1919. Provision of school medical inspection, meals or milk, and the 'nationalising' of hospitals under the Emergency Medical Scheme, can be seen in the same light. Second World War measures for the registering and rehabilitating of the disabled were similarly driven by the need to maximise Britain's labour resources (116). Wars drew attention, too, to the limited technical and other education provided for young workers.

Motives for action were often complex. A sense of obligation to the disadvantaged, of social solidarity, or of duty to the soldier or civilian war-worker, can be identified as inputs to policies adopted. First World War health statistics or, in both wars, scarce or overcrowded housing were accepted as evidence of a deprivation that ought to be put right. The conscript was owed political enfranchisement and material rewards from a grateful country. 'Homes for heroes' and the other reforms planned or considered around the time of the 1918 armistice were not simply a cynical means of buying time for an orderly demobilisation. Similarly, the age and length of service principle which guided Second World War demobilisation was based on natural justice to the individual rather than national economic need, though it has to be admitted that the evidence of 1919 suggested that this was also the only system which was likely to be acceptable to the troops (**39, 76, 116**).

Some of the most significant changes brought about by twentieth-century wars were unplanned. During the First World War, acute labour shortages, particularly in engineering industries, accelerated the development of production-line processes, creating increased opportunities for semi-skilled workers, and serving, when reinforced by government-imposed flat-rate pay awards, to reduce differentials between manual workers of different skills or in different regions and to narrow the gap between 'blue-' and 'white-collar' incomes. Taxation policy during and after both wars, along with new or more generous transfer payments in cash and kind, reinforced, albeit marginally, this process of income equalisation. Rising real incomes, particularly among the lower paid, were the main cause of rising overall health standards.

Though 'full employment' was an object of policy in the period after the Second World War, both the planned and the actual means of achieving this can be seen as unanticipated outcomes of the experience of war. The White Paper 'Employment Policy' and the devices to manage overall and regional levels of employment, adopted by post-war governments, were products of the wartime adoption of Keynesian techniques of economic management, the associated collection and interpretation of statistical data and the development of regulations on investment and building. The actual achievement of high levels of employment was the result of buoyant domestic and world markets for capital and consumer goods, following six years of a war which had diverted the attention of all the major industrial nations, and, though perhaps to a lesser extent, of entrepreneurial confidence in governments' commitment to maintain employment and therefore demand (**110**).

Inter-war unemployment was also, in part, war-related. World over-capacity in textiles, coal-mining, steel-making or shipbuilding was a direct product of war. So was the short-term disruption and impoverishment of much of the European market and the instability born of changes in the structure of international indebtedness. British uncompetitiveness and unemployment were aggravated, in the case of an industry like textiles, by inflation and by the uncontrolled investment boom that followed the peace. At the very least, the First World War accelerated the onset of serious structural and regional unemployment and accentuated the cyclical problem of the periods 1920–22 and 1929–32.

The lack of any marked progress for women in the employment field in the period after the First World War and their contrasting experience after the Second World War followed from these general economic conditions. The slump of 1920–22 completed a process of economic retreat begun even before the 1918 armistice. By contrast, the labour shortage of the 1940s and 50s slowed and then reversed women's withdrawal from employment following the Second World War.

There were other effects of war which might be described as negative or socially divisive. Anti-alien feelings, while not unique to war, were stirred up by the fears and circumstances which war created. Invasion of traditionally male workplaces led, particularly in the First World War, to a heightened hostility to working women. The war of 1914–18 diverted political attention from the issue of the female franchise. The Boer War diverted attention and resources from the issues of old-age pensions and subsidised working-class housing; the wars of 1914–18 and 1939–45 postponed the process of educational reform.

Finally, war led to shifts in the location of political and economic influence and power. The press and, to a lesser extent, film in both wars, along with the wireless in the Second World War, became recognised as powerful manipulators of popular opinion. Trade unions suffered statutory constraints on their liberty of action. However, they gained, at national and plant level, from the full employment that war brought, from the need to maintain production at almost' any cost, and from the negotiations necessary to implement new working arrangements. The advance of political labour in both major wars might be interpreted as a conscious act of policy in the search for the national solidarity that war demanded. On the other hand, the division of the Liberal Party during and after the First

World War was a result of the events of war. Similarly, Labour's achievements after the Second World War were aided by the wartime experience and publicity gained by the party leadership and by the war-related acceptance of government planning and intervention.

There are also, of course, clear continuities in the social history of Britain during the first half of the twentieth century. In some areas of social policy or social structure, wars could be seen as largely irrelevant to a process of long-term evolution, or as producing only short-term or limited interference in this process. Social welfare reform in the areas of education or income maintenance at the end of the First World War can be seen as growing out of measures introduced by Conservative or Liberal governments in the Edwardian era. Similarly, the ideas on which the National Health Service or the 1944 Education Act were based were in circulation long before the war. Beveridge himself stressed the evolution of his insurance proposals from existing practice. Even the infiltration of Keynesianism into the Treasury has been traced back to the 1930s.

In politics, the declining influence of the landed class was already evident before 1914, while much of the base on which organised labour was to build was in place. Though the Liberals were the governing party in 1914, many of the problems of ideology, finance and organisation which were to divide and almost destroy them were also apparent (**67**). The deficiencies in British economic structure, an over-dependence on slow-growing and often badly organised or under-capitalised traditional staples, which lay at the root of inter-war unemployment, also existed prior to 1914. Likewise, the sources of post-Second World War prosperity – high levels of housebuilding, the growth of the motor vehicle, aircraft, chemicals and electrical and electronic engineering industries – were established prior to the Second World War.

Trends in employment were also, up to a point, independent of war. The process of de-skilling in industries such as engineering, and the movement of women into service industry employment, were underway long before the First World War. Conversely, the expansion of the motor vehicle, electrical, aircraft and chemical industries was increasing the demand for skilled labour in the period before 1939.

In other ways, wars might be seen to have had short-term rather than lasting or significant effects, with traditional values or vested interests reasserting themselves once the abnormal circumstances of the conflict had passed. The armed forces changed little as a result of the First World War, though the continuation of conscription into peacetime after 1945 meant that discontinuities were rather more marked after the Second World War. The fate of several social policy measures, including those aimed at achieving an industrial consensus, after the First World War could be seen as an example of this (**24, 44, 50**); the failure of women to maintain employment gains would be another. Calder's case for the frustration of Second World War popular political radicalism is in the same vein, as is Bevan's reference to 'a general lethargy of the collective will' in explaining the limits to post-Second World War social reform (**89, 100**). Society, for both Mowat and Calder, writing respectively of the wars of 1914–18 and 1939–45, settled back into the 'old grooves' (**50, 89**).

Though there have been continuities and instances of short-lived change, twentieth-century wars have clearly distorted historical experience. In some ways, as with the death of loved ones, the experience of bombing or the harassment of aliens, this has been distressing and unpleasant. In other ways, including full employment and better wages or wartime measures to improve nutrition, the effect has been beneficial. War has also created changing priorities and changing perceptions of what might be done. This has led to an acceleration and radicalisation of social policy developments – though, as the fates of post-1918 social legislation or indeed, eventually, the post-1945 health and education services have demonstrated, these measures proved vulnerable once peacetime economic priorities reasserted themselves.

Overall, the war of 1939–45 had a greater and more lasting impact than the Boer or First World War. In part, this was a legacy of earlier events. Popular perceptions of 'broken promises' after 1918 influenced Second World War planners and brought about the election of a Labour government pledged to reform. The planned changes were based, as we have seen, on mixed motives. More important, though, than any plans were the unanticipated consequences of the war, with their effects on social structure and policy alike, notably the prolonged economic boom, contrasting so sharply with the experience of the inter-war years. Twentieth-century wars did not bring social revolution, but even those of 1899–1902 and 1914–18 left, on balance, a positive social legacy, while that of 1939–45 created a vastly more optimistic society, one which at least attempted to establish security and welfare as achievable objectives. If, with hindsight, it is now deemed to have failed, it is in part because of the very ambition of those objectives.

Part Four: Documents

Mafeking Night

After a long period of anticipation, news of the relief of Mafeking finally reached London on the evening of 18 May 1900.

Not Mafeking Day after all but Mafeking Night. And what a night! London was caught off its guard. Deceived by a number of false reports, it had crushed down the fever of unrest and suspense in its mighty bosom and gone about its prosaic concerns. London was at home, at the theatre, the opera, the music hall, preparing for the morrow's business. . . .

Then, unexpectedly, a little after nine-o'clock, the thrilling news was flung out from the newspaper offices on the staid streets – percolated, in some mysterious way, into places of amusement – flashed with magnetic celerity into suburbs and by-ways.

The effect was magical and instantaneous. London and its population were both transformed. A cheer, another and another, and then, where had been silence and quietude, dense crowds blocked seething streets and hoarse, deep-throated cheers sped up to the heavens. . . . The transformation went a step further. London blossomed into flags as if by a clever conjuror's trick. Passengers on the buses waved flags as they sang patriotic songs; people in cabs – and on top, sometimes four to a roof – flourished Union Jacks; windows everywhere sprouted them. And the strains of 'Rule Britannia' and 'God Save the Queen', sung with a conviction and sincerity that brought a lump to the throat, came upon the night air from every point of the compass.

Daily Express, 19 May 1900.

document 2

The fitness of recruits

The Boer War drew attention to the large numbers of would-be recruits rejected by the Army.

The bulk of our soldiers are drawn from the unskilled labour class, and consequently from the stratum of the population living in actual poverty or close to the poverty line. . . . The impairment of vigour and physique among the urban poor is easy to understand when we reflect that, in addition to their only being able to provide themselves with food insufficient in quantity and probably poor in quality, their poverty also entails unhealthy environment e.g. defective housing, overcrowding and insanitary surroundings. Add to this the distress resulting from such causes as want of thrift, illness or death of the breadwinner and alcoholic excess. Further, the physical deterioration caused by inherited or acquired disease must not be forgotten. . . .

The one subject which causes anxiety in the future as regards recruiting is the gradual deterioration of the physique of the working classes from which the bulk of recruits must always be drawn, and, when it is remembered that recruiters are instructed not to submit for medical examination candidates for enlistment unless they are reasonably expected to be passed as fit, we cannot but be struck by the percentage considered unfit for service.

Memorandum from Surgeon-General Sir William Taylor, Director General, Army Medical Service. Appendix 1 to *Report of the Select Inter-Departmental Committee on Physical Deterioration*, Cd 2175 (HMSO, 1904).

document 3

Drink and output

War and the patriotic duty to do nothing to hinder production was a god-send to temperance advocates. Alcoholic drink was weakened and pub open-ing restricted. Even so, shipbuilding employers blamed drinking for low output.

It was stated that, in many areas, the number of hours being worked by the men was actually less than before the war. . . . Although working night and day seven days a week, less productiveness was being secured from the men. . . . The deputation was of the opinion that this was principally due to the question of drink. There were many men doing splendid and strenuous work, probably as good as the men in the trenches, but so many were not working anything like full hours and the average was thus disastrously reduced. The members of the deputation stated that they believed that 80% of the present avoidable loss of time could be ascribed to no other cause but drink. . . . the important factor was not the average time worked, but the time worked by certain of the most important branches. In one yard, for example, the riveters had only been working, on the average, 40 hours a week, and in another yard only 36 hours.

Curtailment resulted in excessive drinking during the shortened hours. The takings of certain public houses which had their hours reduced from ten to nine had actually increased.

Statement by a deputation representing the Shipbuilding Employers Federation to D. Lloyd George, Chancellor of the Exchequer, 23 March 1915, *British Temperance Advocate*, May 1915.

document 4

Anti-German riots

The sinking of the Lusitania, *in May 1915, was followed by anti-German riots in East London and elsewhere.*

The loss of the great Cunard liner, the *Lusitania*, was a shock to the world. . . . There was a fierce clamour for reprisals. The meanest elements among the jingoes worked up the first of the anti-German riots. These were deliberately organised, in no sense a spontaneous popular outburst; but the prospect of looting without fear of punishment made its appeal to certain sections of the poor and ignorant. Many a home was wrecked; many a peaceable working family lost its all. Stones were flung, children injured.

Mrs Nuess, an English woman married to a German, a good voluntary worker . . . saw her home utterly dismantled, even to the tools, so costly and so essential, by which her industrious husband and son earned their living as cabinet-makers. She saw her husband, her son and her daughter dragged out of the house by the mob. A day of agonised suspense elapsed before they were able to rejoin her.

On May 13th orders were given for the arrest of all alien enemies (sic) of military age. The ostensible object of the rioting had been achieved. Niederhofer, our big, kind fellow at the factory, had never been molested, not a window of his house was broken. He, too, was arrested and sent to Knockeloe internment camp in the Isle of Man. He was held till the close of the war.

Sylvia Pankhurst, *The Home Front* (Hutchinson, 1932).

document 5

An appeal to the unions

Munitions demanded a greatly expanded and more flexible workforce. Here, Lloyd George calls for union co-operation.

Let me say this, as far as the official representatives of organised labour are concerned we have had nothing but help . . . the difficulty has been when you get beyond. I am not saying a word about Trades Union regulations during a period of peace. I have no doubt they were essential safeguards to protect labour against what otherwise might have been a serious interference with their rights and with their prospects. But . . . Government regulations have to be suspended during the period of the war because they are inapplicable in a time of emergency. The same thing applies to many Trade Union regulations and practices. . . . I should like to call attention to those rules which had been set up, for very good reasons, to make it difficult for unskilled men to claim the position and rights of men who have had training. . . . If all the skilled engineers in this country were turned on to produce what is required, if you brought back from the front every engineer who had been recruited, if you worked them to the utmost limits of human endurance, you have not enough labour even then to produce all we are going to ask you to produce during the next few months. Therefore we must appeal to the patriotism of the unions of this country to relax these particular rules in order to eke out, as it were, the skill . . . to enable us to turn out the necessary munitions of war to win a real and speedy triumph. . . .

D. Lloyd George, speech at Liverpool, 14 June 1915, reproduced in *Through Terror to Triumph* (Hodder and Stoughton, 1915).

document 6
Conscription and the labour movement

The introduction of military conscription divided the labour movement, not least because of the fear that industrial conscription would follow. Beatrice Webb was a strong critic of the measure and of the Labour leaders' acquiescence in it.

January 2nd 1916 The year opens badly for Labour. The Munitions Act and the Defence of the Realm Act, together with the suppression of a free press, has been followed by the Cabinet's decision in favour of compulsory military service. This decision is the last of a series of cleverly devised steps – each step seeming at once harmless and inevitable, even to the opponents of compulsion, but in fact necessitating the next step forward to a system of military and industrial conscription. The Labour members were swept into the movement by the Derby recruiting campaign, and were cajoled, bribed and flattered into accepting the Asquith pledge. The proposed measure seems a small one and affects exactly those persons who have the least strength to resist – the unmarried men of the unorganised industries. . . . But it is obvious that if the war continues, the married men will have to go into the trenches, and directly the Minister of Munitions dares to do it, industrial conscription will be introduced into the whole of industry. The Servile State will have been established.

Margaret Cole (ed.), *Beatrice Webb's Diaries, 1912–1924* (Longmans, Green and Co., 1952).

document 7
Not pulling their weight

Middle-class women with time to window-shop were seen as 'not doing their bit'. Here, on the 'Ladies' Page' of a magazine for the upper and middle classes, they are defended and the attack is turned on working-class women.

There is a good deal of criticism of women 'shop-gazing' in the large towns, especially in the West End of London. It is really the most inexpensive of diversions, provided it does not lead to unnecessary or extravagant buying. . . . But it is said, those women round the shop-windows are wasting time in which they might be making munitions, or setting free others – their servants and needlewomen – to go and make munitions. We must remember that the majority of the 'shop-gazing' women are probably workers in the home. The work of women in the home is indispensable and genuine, but while it goes on intermittently all day, from early morn to bedtime, still there are intervals; and the women whom one sees 'shop-gazing' in the afternoons have usually done some work and will go home to do more, but take this diversion in between home duties, or as part of the brief open-air exercise that is needed by the domestic worker for health. There is, none the less, room for more energy and working spirit on the part of a great many women. The separation allowances to women of the working class, for one thing, have enormously reduced the supply of those willing to go out and earn money by cleaning house. Go to a working-class street to seek a charwoman; each 'lady' thinks 'the lady next door' may like to come.

Illustrated London News, 13 January 1917.

document 8

War and young people

Early school-leaving, high wartime wages, and the absence of fathers from the home were seen as contributing to a serious social problem.

Many children have been withdrawn at an even earlier age than usual from day schools. . . . We are not prepared to say that much of the work which is now being done by juveniles in munitions factories and elsewhere is in itself inferior to the work which most of them would have been doing in normal times, but there can be no doubt that many of the tendencies affecting character and efficiency have incidentally been accentuated. Unsuitable occupations in the distributive trades have largely been transferred from boys to girls. Parental control, so far as it formerly existed, has been relaxed, largely through the absence of fathers. . . . Wages have been exceptionally high, and although this has led to an improved standard of living, it has also, in ill-regulated households, induced habits of foolish and mischievous extravagance. Even the ordinary discipline of the workshop has in varying degrees given way; while the withdrawal of influences making for the social improvement of boys and girls has in many districts been followed by noticeable deterioration in behaviour and morality. Gambling has increased. Excessive hours of strenuous labour have overtaxed the powers of young people;

while many have taken advantage of the extraordinary demand for juvenile labour to change even more rapidly from one blind alley employment to another.

Final Report of the Departmental Committee on Juvenile Education in Relation to Employment after the War, Cd 8512 (HMSO, 1917).

document 9
The cost of living and industrial unrest

In Scotland, the industrial disturbances of the spring of 1917 were blamed on the increased cost of living and on profiteering.

There is no doubt that the chief, and fundamental, cause of the existing unrest is the increased cost of living, which, in the minds of workers, is the result of the Government having failed effectively to control the production, supply and distribution of food, and thus opened the door to what the worker terms 'profiteering'. No doubt wages have been greatly advanced, but the feeling of the general body of workers is that wages, not having advanced corresponding to the increased cost of living, the worker is really worse off than before the war, instead of being greatly better off as is frequently supposed. There are indications . . . the aggregate weekly incomes of industrial workers keep pace with the cost of living, a conclusion which seems supported by the knowledge of the large amount of overtime worked, of the large amount of money paid to women workers not previously engaged on industry, of the numerous families in receipt of separation allowances and sums from the soldiers' and sailors' funds and other agencies. The grievance of the workers is not so much in regard to the money coming in, but rather that the increased receipts (in many cases arising from increased exertion or prolonged hours of work) are absorbed by increased living costs, a state of affairs which they believe to be owing to certain privileged classes not sharing in the general sacrifice and indeed profiting by the sacrifice of others.

Commission of Enquiry into the Industrial Unrest, Report of the Commissioners for Scotland, Cd 8669 (HMSO, 1917).

Maternity and child welfare

The First World War gave a further incentive to the movement for improving the health of mothers and infants.

The war has had the effect of directing greatly increased attention to means for improving the health of mothers and of their children during the first five years of life. During 1916, work with this object has been much increased, though some local authorities still remain inert, and appear to be unwilling to realise that the truest national economy can only be secured by saving life and procuring health by all practicable means.

The need for increased effort to save child life is shown by the markedly lower natural increase of population in 1916 than in 1914. In the year 1914 there were 362,354 more births than deaths in England and Wales. In the year 1915 this excess of births over deaths was only 252,201. In the year 1916, the corresponding excess of births over deaths was 277,227, there being 29,073 fewer births and 54,099 fewer deaths than in 1915.

The reduction in the number of births emphasises the importance of saving child life and improving the health of all survivors. There is no insuperable difficulty in reducing the total deaths in childhood to one-half their present number.

It is noteworthy that during 1916 the rate of infant mortality was the lowest on record.

Forty-sixth Annual Report of the Local Government Board: Supplement containing the Report of the Medical Officer for 1916–17, Cd 8767 (HMSO, 1917).

Factory welfare

Wartime munitions employment, particularly that of women, led to significant advances in factory welfare facilities.

Previously to the war, welfare arrangements were enforced by the Home Office, particularly in the case of certain unhealthy industries [such] as the pottery trade, and were adopted voluntarily by a certain number of enlightened employers in other trades; but no extensive development took place until the emergency conditions arising out of the war, notably the employment at night of large numbers of women, brought about a widespread recognition of the need of additional arrangements for the comfort and well-being of the workers. As a result of the combined efforts of the Factory Department of the Home Office and of the Health and Welfare Department of the Ministry of Munitions, which was specially established for the purpose, and with the ready co-operation of the general body of employers, a great change has been effected and a new standard of surroundings has been created both in national and controlled establishments where over 2,000,000 workers are employed, and in large numbers of other works belonging to non-munition industries. In this work invaluable assistance has been rendered by the Health of Munitions Workers Committee which, by the issue of memoranda tracing the effect upon output of length of hours, *dietary* [sic], systems of payment, amenities of factory accommodation, and intelligent and sympathetic supervision of the workers has given great stimulus to the welfare movement and has helped guide it on satisfactory and progressive lines.

War Cabinet, Report for the Year 1917, Cd 9005 (HMSO, 1918).

document 12

Educational reform and its opponents

Fisher's Education bills met with opposition. A Times *leader on the second bill, of January 1918, shows that, while he had won over the local authorities, Fisher was still opposed by employers.*

It may seem strange that Parliament, at this crisis, agrees to devote . . . time to a measure which is not claimed . . . to be capable of influencing the course of the war during the present year. Yet it is probable that the historian . . . will find in our present interest in education some evidence of that length of view which distinguishes the statesman from the opportunist. Confident in our strength to win by the union of might with right, the historian may record, we found time, even amid the anxieties of a dark hour, to prepare to make victory worthwhile.

It would be a mistake, however, to think that . . . the Bill will have a smooth passage . . . into law . . . the industrial opposition has still to be faced. This comes from two sources. Some employers believe that the abolition of child labour will prove to be an intolerable handicap to our economic future, and some working-class opinion fears the withdrawal of children's wages from the family income. We believe, on the contrary, that in the long run educated workers are not only happier, but more profitable both to themselves and to their employer, and that the existence of child labour lessens men's wages both in weekly amount and in the period of years over which they are spread. We believe, moreover, that the majority of enlightened employers share our view, and there is complete evidence that organised labour does so.

The Times, 26 February 1918.

document 13

Addison versus the Treasury

The unexpectedly rapid collapse of the German armies in the late summer and autumn of 1918 led to the need for quick decisions by those planning the peace. At the end of October, Christopher Addison (Minister of Reconstruction) was trying to secure an adequate level of benefit for those demobilised servicemen and civilians who were unable to find work.

The Treasury sent a deputation across to me on Thursday evening, the 31st, at which their chief spokesman was in his most insolent mood at my proposed scale for out-of-work benefit, which was 20/- a week for men – five-sixths of that amount for women – and 7/6 for one dependent child and 1/6 each other child. He suggested that the Treasury might possibly concede up to 14/- for the man. By this time I was in a pugilistic mood and told him that if he were to go to the Tommies in the trenches and tell them he thought 14/- would be enough for them to live on if they could not get a job after demobilisation, he would probably be strung up to the nearest post and would deserve it.

Christopher Addison, *Four and a Half Years*, vol. II (Hutchinson, 1934).

document 14

Winning the peace

On the day after the armistice, Lloyd George urged his Liberal supporters to make victory a platform for social reform.

The Prime Minister said: The first thing to avoid is the fatal example which was set in 1815 when advantage was taken of victory to deny reform. . . . Rather let us utilise victory to get the necessary impetus for reform! We must instantly take in hand an improvement of the conditions of the people. He spoke of the light which recruiting statistics had thrown upon the health of the manhood of the country. . . .

The Prime Minister spoke of the need of a great housing programme, and of bringing light and beauty into the lives of the people. He said: We must have habitations fit for the heroes who have won the war. He spoke with great sympathy of the conditions of labour, of wages, and of a reduction in the hours of labour. He indicated the necessity for a minimum wage which would ensure to every honest worker a decent standard of life.

The Prime Minister referred to the revolutionary spirit which was in the air. He said: Properly used, there is value in that spirit. . . . What it needs is wise direction. The revolutionary spirit must be combated with the spirit which has won the war – the spirit of national unity, of co-operation, of sacrifice. If that spirit can be preserved for five years, the face of the country will be transformed. Revolution I am not afraid of. Bolshevism I am not afraid of. It is reaction that I am afraid of. Yes, reaction and disunion.

The Times, 13 November 1918.

document 15

Internment

Defeat in France led to fears of invasion and a harsher policy with regard to enemy aliens.

Three thousand five hundred women enemy aliens were interned yesterday. Police acted swiftly on a sudden order from the Home Office and many of the women were still in bed when the police walked in.

Most of them will be sent to comfortable billets in the Isle of Man, where landladies will look after them. They will have a great deal of freedom, except that they will not be allowed out of the town in which they are interned.

The women are Germans and Austrians between the ages of sixteen and sixty. Those who have children under sixteen will be allowed to take them along.

All the women in this new round-up are those who held a 'B'

certificate – that is, they were exempt from internment, but their movements were restricted and they were not allowed to have cameras or cars.

More than 1,500 of them lived in London; usually domestic servants and nursemaids. . . . The women were taken in cars to the nearest police station to await further instructions. By noon, several hundred women had been taken from the police stations in patrol wagons and private cars to special places in London.

The total number of aliens now interned in Britain is 10,000.

Daily Mirror, 28 May 1940.

document 16

Doing better than last time

J. B. Priestley's 'Postscripts' followed the nine-o'clock news on Sunday nights in the summer of 1940. His message, however, aroused opposition in some quarters for being too political.

I will tell you what we did for [servicemen] and their young wives at the end of the last war. We did nothing – except let them take their chance in a world where every gangster and trickster and stupid insensitive fool or rogue was let loose to do his damnedest. After the cheering and the flag-waving was over, and all the medals were given out, somehow the young heroes disappeared, but after a year or two there were a lot of shabby, young-oldish men about who didn't seem to have been lucky in the scramble for easy jobs and quick profits. . . .

No doubt, it's going to be all different this time, but . . . the same kinds of minds are still about. Among bundles of very friendly letters just lately I've been getting some very fierce and angry ones telling me to get off the air before the Government 'puts you where you belong' – the real Fascist touch. Well, obviously, it wouldn't matter very much if I were taken off the air, but it would matter a great deal, even to these Blimps, if [the] young men of the R.A.F. were taken off the air; and so I repeat my question – in return for their skill, devotion, endurance and self-sacrifice, what are we civilians prepared to do? . . . the least we can do is to give our minds honestly, sincerely and without immediate self-interest, to the task of preparing a world really fit for them and their kind – to arrange a final 'happy landing'.

J. B. Priestley, 'Postscript', 28 July 1940.

document 17

Bombing and social disruption

Contrary to expectations, civilian populations proved able to endure bombing, but the strain and stress was considerable.

It is not so much that the bombing is worrying in itself as that the disorganisation of traffic, frequent difficulty of telephoning, shutting of shops whenever there is a raid on . . . combined with the necessity of getting on with one's ordinary work, wear one out and turn life into a constant scramble to catch up lost time. . . .

The delayed action bombs are a great nuisance. . . . All over South London, little groups of disconsolate-looking people wandering about with suitcases and bundles, either people who have been rendered homeless or, in more cases, who have been turned out by the authorities because of an unexploded bomb. . . .

Most of last night in the public shelter, having been driven there by recurrent whistle and crash of bombs not very far away at intervals of about a quarter of an hour. Frightful discomfort owing to overcrowding, though the place was well-appointed with electric light and fans. People, mostly elderly working-class, grousing bitterly about the hardness of the seats and the longness of the night, but no defeatist talk.

George Orwell, wartime diary, 10 September 1940, in S. Orwell and I. Angus (eds), *The Collected Essays, Journalism and Letters of George Orwell*, vol. II, *My Country Right or Left 1940–1943* (Secker and Warburg, 1968).

document 18

Bombing: the personal impact

Nella Last, a Barrow housewife, described her experiences and emotions during and after a bombing attack which quite badly damaged her home.

Sunday 4th May 1941
A night of terror, and there are few windows left in the district – or roof tiles! Land mines, incendiaries and explosives were dropped, and we cowered thankfully under our indoor shelter. I've been so dreadfully sick all day, and I'm sure it's sheer fright, for last night I really thought our end had come. . . . I've a sick shadow over me as I look at my loved little house that will never be the same again.

The windows are nearly all out, the metal frames strained, the ceilings down, the walls cracked and the garage roof showing four inches of daylight where it joins the wall. Doors are splintered and off – and there is the dirt from the blast that swept down the chimney. The house rocked and then the kitchenette door careered down the hall and plaster showered on the shelter. I'll never forget my odd sensations, one a calm acceptance of 'the end', the other a feeling of regret that I'd not opened a tin of fruit salad for tea – and now it was too late!

R. Broad and S. Fleming (eds), *Nella Last's War* (Falling Wall Press, 1981).

document 19

Rationing for some

Rationing never applied to restaurants. Here the Daily Mirror *attacks the inequity that this led to.*

Lord Woolton, Food Minister, warned Britain again yesterday: 'The position of meat supplies is immediately difficult . . . if we find we cannot live up to the ls 6d ration we shall reduce it.'

But if you have money you can say 'To Hell with Rations', laugh at food coupons – and eat as much rationed food as you wish. . . . The Cabinet, fully aware of this national scandal, has neglected to tackle it. . . . Now they must act. It is a problem easily solved. Introduce coupons for all restaurant meals and see that nobody gets more than his share. The nation demands it.

Cassandra reveals how easy it is to gorge without coupons.

Within five days I have eaten at least seven times my weekly meat ration, five times my bacon ration, nearly half a pound of butter, and have had so much sugar I couldn't eat it all. . . .

Not content with this debauch, I have swallowed saddle of hare in wine sauce, lobster thermidor, the inevitable (if you live that way!) caviare, Hungarian pork goulash, quails in aspic and truffled goose livers. . . .

This Everest of food has been obtained without the loss of a single food coupon. My stomach is stunned. Without regard to cost, it has fought in the grill rooms, in the restaurants, in the dives, in the butteries and in the buffets. . . .

Daily Mirror, 8 January 1941.

document 20

Banning the *Daily Worker*

In January 1941, Herbert Morrison, the Home Secretary, banned publication of the Daily Worker *which was opposing the war. This* Daily Mirror *editorial argues, perhaps with prescience, that this was the wrong policy.*

The Home Secretary, Mr Herbert Morrison, has decided on two points. . . . One is that the Stalinite daily no-newspaper, calling itself *The Daily Worker*, is a newspaper of no importance. The other is that *The Daily Worker* is important enough to be suppressed. And these two points and that decision apply also to Mr Claude Pitcairn Cockburn's lively little leaflet *The Week* – or, as we prefer to call it, *The Squeak*.

Frankly we cannot believe that either of these publications has much influence in this country. The question for the Home Secretary, as for all men appointed to watch public opinion, is whether a dead *Daily Worker* will not have much greater influence than one allowed to go on living in a moribund condition of prolonged tedium. In other words, is not Mr Morrison making martyrs? And are not martyrs magnificent advertising agents for any cause?

The so-called communists will be delighted. They now have something to squeak about. They will squeak at street corners or surreptitiously. It is a grand day for them.

Apart from that . . . all suppression of opinion as opposed to falsified fact is dangerous. This is a dangerous precedent.

Daily Mirror, 22 January 1941.

document 21

Shortages

The war effort meant cutbacks in production of goods for civilian use. The scale of the cuts varied according to availability of materials, or judgements on need or importance to morale.

Supplies of Articles for Civilian Use in the United Kingdom

	1935 Millions	1943 Millions
Boots and shoes	161	90
Stockings and socks (pairs)	390	240
Armchairs and settees	2.7	0.1
Woollen blankets	6.5	2.2
Wool carpets and rugs } Square yards	34	1.5
Linoleum etc.	92	14
Vacuum cleaners	0.4	–
Household brushes and brooms	60	25
Table knives	24	4
Ladies' handbags	10	1
Watches	6.5	0.3
Matches (boxes of 50)	2,750	1,700
Football bladders	1.5	0.1
Golf balls	7	–

	Thousands	Thousands
Motor cars	280	–
Bicycles and Tricycles	1,600	540
Perambulators, folders & pushchairs	590	410
Wireless receiving sets	1,900	50
Wireless valves for replacements	5,000	3,500
Gramophone records	20,000	11,000

Statistics Relating to the War Effort of the United Kingdom, Cmd 6564 (HMSO, 1944).

document 22

Planning the peace

On 4 January 1941, Picture Post published a series of articles on the sort of future which could be created. Thomas Balogh wrote on the means of finding work for all.

The most important thing is to realise that the end of the war will not be the time to return to what used to be called 'normal' – that is, complete freedom for the speculator to make high profits out of the world's need of reconstruction. On the contrary, the reconstruction ought to be planned exactly as war production ought to be planned. Just as Government controls are needed at present to enable the nation to throw its whole strength into the war effort, so a system of Government controls – reformed both in character and personnel – is needed to enable us to throw our whole strength into the peace effort. Manpower must be controlled so it can be directed where it is most needed, and demobilisation must take place not as it did last time – when millions of men were thrown on to the labour market – but according to the work which can be provided. The supply of materials must be adjusted according to the task. In fact, we must have a national plan of reconstruction. Now the word 'plan' is somewhat unpopular, especially because it denotes a certain amount of compulsion or direction which is not favoured by a freedom-loving people. But we have surely reached the stage of overcoming this prejudice, which has been fostered by the people who want freedom to profit at the expense of the majority.

Thomas Balogh, 'Work for All', *Picture Post*, 4 January 1941.

document 23

Lack of enthusiasm for Beveridge's scheme

Not everyone was enthusiastic for Beveridge's plans. Those representing the British Employers Confederation said as much to the Committee on Social Insurance and Allied Services.

Sir John Forbes Watson We think that this Committee has done a useful piece of work but we do not think that this country is waiting to hear what this Committee says; it is waiting to know what is happening to our Army and our Navy and our Air Force today . . . and the social services . . . are not matters that keep us off our sleep at nights.

Mr Boyd We are not suggesting that we or you should forget the social services or the post-war position. I think perhaps some of us recognise that there are factors at work which are rather difficult to put on paper . . . things which are said in relation to morale, things related directly to winning the war, but to jump from that step to the next step and to think you can lay down in any precise form at all what is to happen after the war is something we are not prepared to do. I think most of us feel that there may have been excellent reasons in the last war for talking about homes for heroes and there may be excellent reasons today for talking about improving the social services, but . . . problems after the war are not problems that the man in the street concerns himself about, and you may be causing a much greater degree of danger by telling him something in fact even the most optimistic of us fear will be impossible.

Minutes of Evidence to the Committee on Social Insurance and Allied Services, 11th Meeting, Part 2, 20 May 1942, PRO CAB 87/77.

document 24

War for peace

William Beveridge argued that the balance of advantage lay in planning for peace while the war continued.

There are difficulties in planning reconstruction of the social services during the height of war, but there are also advantages in doing so. The prevention of want and the diminution and relief of distress – the special aim of the social services – are in fact a common interest of all citizens. It may be possible to secure a keener realisation of that fact in war than it is in peace, because war breeds national unity. It may be possible, through sense of national unity and readiness to sacrifice personal interests to the common cause, to bring about changes which, when they are made, will be accepted on all hands as advances, but which it might be difficult to make at other times. There appears at any rate to be no doubt of the determination of the British people, however hard pressed in war, not to live wholly for war, not to abandon care of what may come after. That, after all, is in accord with the nature of democracies, of the spirit in which they fight and of the purpose for which they fight. They make war, today more consciously than ever, not for the sake of war, not for dominion or revenge, but war for peace.

William Beveridge, *Social Insurance and Allied Services*, Cmd 6404 (HMSO, November 1942).

document 25

The government's dilemma

Beveridge 'leaked' his proposals prior to publication, in a bid to force the government's hand. Lord Cherwell, Chief Scientific Adviser to the government and a confidant of Churchill, indicated the difficulties in accepting or rejecting Beveridge's scheme.

The real difficulty in accepting this scheme now is that it only covers part of our post-war economic arrangement. It is very difficult to see how these will work out until we have finished our discussions with America. We shall be bound to ask them for a good deal of assistance – Lease/Lend and perhaps gold – quite apart from concessions in export markets. It may be that acceptance of this scheme would be used against us in the U.S.A. where people might be told they were being asked to pay for social services in the U.K. far in advance of their own.

On the other hand, there has unfortunately been so much carefully engineered advanced publicity that the Government's hand may have been forced. In my view a scheme on some such lines might be welcomed as an ultimate objective. But as things have turned out we seem to be faced, owing to the improper leakages and reports which have been sedulously circulated, with the alternatives of possibly unhappy repercussions in America if we accept it or of political difficulty here if we don't.

Cherwell to Prime Minister, 25 November 1942, PRO PREM 4/89/2.

document 26
Individual opportunity and national need

Though the White Paper 'Educational Reconstruction' was well received, it was not especially radical in its proposals. Diversity of opportunity was to be as important as equality and the stress was on youth as a national asset.

The Government's purpose in putting forward the reforms described in this Paper is to secure for children a happier childhood and a better start in life; to ensure a fuller measure of education and opportunity for young people and to provide means for all of developing the various talents with which they are endowed and so enriching the inheritance of the country whose citizens they are. The new educational opportunities must not, therefore, be of a single pattern. It is just as important to achieve diversity as it is equality of educational opportunity. But such diversity must not impair the social unity within the educational system which will open the way to a more closely knit society and give us strength to face the tasks ahead. The war has revealed afresh the character and resources of the British people – an enduring possession that will survive all the material losses inevitable in the present struggle. In the youth of the nation we have our greatest national asset. Even on a basis of mere expediency, we cannot afford not to develop this asset to the greatest advantage. It is the object of the present proposals to strengthen and inspire the younger generation. For it is as true today, as when it was first said, that 'the bulwarks of a city are its men'.

Educational Reconstruction, Cmd 6458 (HMSO, July 1943).

document 27

Worries about the peace

As the end of the war approached, there was increasing concern that the government should attend to housing needs. The polls of the British Institute of Public Opinion, published in the News Chronicle, *demonstrate this trend.*

August 1944: If you had to say which question should be tackled the very first by the government returned at the general election, what would it be?

Housing	39%
Employment	29%
Food Shortages	1%
Cost of Living	3%
Export Trade	1%
Demobilisation	2%
Education	1%
Nationalisation of Industry	1%
Finance	1%
Health	1%
Treatment of Germany, Japan	1%
Other problems	8%
No opinion	5%

February 1945: What do you think is the most urgent home-front problem that the government must solve during the next few months?

Housing	54%
Employment	13%
Cost of Living	1%
Social Security; pensions	2%
Coal Crisis	4%
Preparation for return of forces	4%
Switch-over to peace production	3%
Other problems	12%
No opinion	7%

G. H. Gallup (ed.), *The Gallup International Public Opinion Polls: Great Britain 1937–1975* (Random House, 1976).

document 28
Conservatives and housing

Conservative plans for social reconstruction were incorporated in a series of pamphlets under the collective title 'Looking Ahead'.

Anyone in England today knows how hard it is to find a house. The parents of children usually have the longest search for a house, and even the single person finds it difficult to obtain lodging. It is the duty of all of us to put this matter right by seeing that in the shortest possible time after the war is won there is a home for every family throughout the United Kingdom. This can be done; but not without . . . straight thinking, hard work and some sacrifices. All these were essential to the long build-up of the munitions programme which brings victory to our arms; no less are they vital in the battles already being fought for peace, against poverty, ill-health and homelessness.

The years of war have brought grave consequences to housing. Many houses have been – and may yet be – destroyed by enemy action, while the normal replacement of old and unfit dwellings . . . has been halted since its outbreak . . . we shall divide our programme into three parts. . . . During the emergency period our urgent task must be to provide shelter for the entire population. In the intermediate period, we must concentrate on slum clearance and the relief of overcrowding. . . . In the long-term period, once there is a habitable house for every family in the country . . . we can proceed to improve the quality of our housing by the steady replacement of old houses by new.

Conservative Central Committee on Post-war Reconstruction, *A Policy for Housing in England and Wales* (January 1945).

document 29
A woman welcomes the opportunity for part-time work

Mass-Observation revealed that, while women doing full-time war work often found it a heavy burden, those in part-time jobs found them psychologically and economically rewarding. A 40-year-old mother of two had this to say:

I came here through patriotic motives. I had no need to work. One of my children is evacuated but one is at home. My husband is in the Civil Service. I think I'm very lucky, that's the reason I came here. When the war's over the job will be somebody else's who's been in the forces. But I thoroughly enjoy my four hours working in the afternoon. I'm all agog to get here. After all, for a housewife who's been a cabbage for fifteen years – you feel you've got out of the cage and you're free. Quite a lot of part-timers feel like that – to get out and see some fresh faces – it's all so different, such a change from dusting. I think the war has made a lot of difference to housewives. I don't think they'll want to go back to the old narrow life. Another thing, they enjoy earning a little money for themselves, of their own, even if it all goes on the children. I have the feeling myself that I've got to go back into the home. I wouldn't like to keep any man out of a job, but I do hope there'll be more part-time jobs going after the war.

Mass-Observation, *The Journey Home* (Advertising Services Guild, 1944).

document 30

A people's victory

Labour feared that Churchill's achievements as a war leader would lead to a Conservative victory in the 1945 election. The party sought to establish the war as a people's victory and to warn against a people's defeat in the peace to follow.

So far as Britain's contribution is concerned, this war will have been won by its people, not by any one man or set of men, though strong and greatly valued leadership has been given to the resolve of the people in the present struggle. And in this leadership, the Labour Ministers have taken their full share of burdens and responsibilities. . . .

The people made tremendous efforts to win the last war also. But when they had won it they lacked a lively interest in the social and economic problems of peace, and accepted the election promises of the leaders of the anti-Labour parties at their face value. So the 'hard-faced men who had done well out of the war' were able to get the kind of peace that suited themselves. The people lost that peace. And when we say 'peace' we mean not only the Treaty, but the social and economic policy which followed the fighting.

The Labour Party makes no baseless promises. The future will not be easy. But this time the peace must be won. The Labour Party offers the nation a plan which will win the Peace for the People.

Let us Face the Future (Labour Party Election Manifesto, 1945).

Glossary

People

Clement Attlee Leader of the Parliamentary Labour Party and member of Churchill's Coalition government; Deputy Prime Minister, 1943–45.

Ernest Bevin Trade union leader and Minister of Labour and National Service in Churchill's Coalition government.

Stafford Cripps Socialist and MP, expelled from the Labour Party in 1938. Ambassador to Moscow, 1940–42; Leader of the Commons, 1942; Minister of Aircraft Production, 1942–45.

Hugh Dalton Labour MP, President of the Board of Trade, 1942–45.

Margaret Macmillan Socialist and pioneer of medical inspection and treatment for schoolchildren.

Robert Morant Civil servant, successively Permanent Secretary at Board of Education, 1903–11; Chairman of the National Health Insurance Commission, 1911–19; Permanent Secretary at the Ministry of Health, 1919–20.

Herbert Morrison Labour MP, Home Secretary in Churchill's Coalition government.

Sidney and Beatrice Webb Fabian socialists, influential in the development of social welfare provision by central and local government.

Subjects

Approved societies Industrial assurance societies and friendly societies approved to operate the Health Insurance Scheme established under the 1911 Act.

Atlantic Charter Statement of war aims resulting from meeting between Churchill and Roosevelt on a battleship off Newfoundland in August 1940.

Emergency Hospital Scheme Otherwise known as Emergency Medical Service. Government-run hospital service established at the outbreak of the Second World War; this involved the takeover and rationalisation of much local authority and voluntary provision.

117

'Garden city' designs Low-density, well-equipped housing providing a healthy living environment. Derived from the ideas of Ebenezer Howard and implemented in the early years of the century at Letchworth Garden City.

Guardians Elected bodies responsible for administering the Poor Law.

'If the Invader Comes' (1940) Ministry of Information leaflet on what to do in the event of invasion, issued to every household in June 1940.

Mass-Observation Organisation founded in 1937 to discover the attitudes and lifestyles of ordinary people.

Mulberry harbour Prefabricated harbour, constructed in Britain and towed across the Channel to provide landing facilities for supplies and equipment following D-Day, 1944.

National Industrial Conference (1919) Government-sponsored meetings of representatives of employers and trade unions.

November 1918 'coupon' election So called because of the letter of endorsement ('coupon'), jointly signed by Lloyd George (Liberal) and Bonar Law (Conservative), given to those candidates who had supported the government in the 'Maurice debate' (May 1918) against the charge that it had dangerously weakened British forces on the western front.

Pooling of panel work A system whereby GPs treating 'panel' (i.e., National Health Insurance Scheme) patients operated a rota, or established district centres, to cover one another's patients or those of colleagues in the forces. Income from the panel patients was pooled and shared out among the practices involved.

Wartime Social Survey Government-sponsored quantitative research into public opinion, set up in 1940 under the supervision of the London School of Economics.

'Zec shipwrecked sailor cartoon' Published in the *Daily Mirror* on 6 March 1942, showing a shipwrecked sailor clinging to a raft and bearing the caption 'The price of petrol has been increased by one penny – Official' (see cover).

Bibliography

GENERAL WORKS DEALING WITH WAR OR TWENTIETH-CENTURY
HISTORY

1 D. Aldcroft, *The British Economy*, Vol. 1, *The Years of Turmoil, 1920–1951* (Harvester, 1986)

2 S. Andreski, *Military Organisation and Society* (Routledge and Kegan Paul, 1968 edn.)

3 R. Barker, *Education and Politics, 1900–1951* (Oxford University Press, 1972)

4 I. F. W. Beckett, 'Total War' in C. McInnes and G. Sheffield (eds), *Warfare in the Twentieth Century* (Unwin Hyman, 1988)

5 M. Beloff, *Wars and Welfare: Britain 1914–1945* (Edward Arnold, 1984)

6 B. Bond, *War and Society in Europe, 1870–1970* (Fontana, 1984)

7 G. Braybon and P. Summerfield, *Out of the Cage* (Pandora, 1987)

8 D. Fraser, *The Evolution of the British Welfare State* (Macmillan, 1984 edn.)

9 A. H. Halsey, *Trends in British Society since 1900* (Macmillan, 1972)

10 J. Harris, *William Beveridge: A Biography* (Oxford University Press, 1977)

11 C. E. V. Leser, 'Men and Women in Industry', *Economic Journal*, lxii, 1952

12 J. Lewis, *Women in England, 1870–1950* (Wheatsheaf, 1984)

13 T. H. Marshall, *Social Policy* (Hutchinson, 1975 edn.)

14 A. Marwick, *Britain in the Century of Total War* (Bodley Head, 1968)

15 A. Marwick, *War and Social Change in the Twentieth Century* (Macmillan, 1974)

16 A. Marwick, *The Four-tier Model Revisited* (Open University Press, 1978)

17 A. Marwick (ed.), *Total War and Social Change* (Macmillan, 1988)

18 K. Middlemass, *Politics and Industry* (André Deutsch, 1979)

19 A. Milward, *The Economic Effects of the World Wars on Britain* (Macmillan, 1970)

20 S. Pollard, *The Development of the British Economy, 1914–1980* (Edward Arnold, 1983)

21 A. J. P. Taylor, *English History 1914–1945* (Oxford University Press, 1965)

22 P. Thane, *The Foundations of the Welfare State* (Longman, 1982)

23 R. M. Titmuss, 'War and Social Policy', *Essays on the Welfare State* (Allen and Unwin, 1955)

WORKS DEALING WITH THE BOER AND FIRST WORLD WARS

24 P. Abrams, 'The Failure of Social Reform, 1918–20', *Past and Present*, xxix, 1963

25 L. Andrews, *The Education Act, 1918* (Routledge and Kegan Paul, 1976)

26 S. Armitage, *The Politics of Decontrol of Industry: Britain and the United States* (Weidenfeld and Nicolson, 1969)

27 I. F. W. Beckett and K. Simpson (eds), *A Nation in Arms: A Social Study of the British Army in the First World War* (Manchester University Press, 1985)

28 R. Bourne, *Britain and the Great War, 1914–1918* (Edward Arnold, 1989)

29 G. Braybon, *Women Workers in the First World War* (Croom Helm, 1981)

30 K. Burk, *War and the State* (Allen and Unwin, 1982)

31 J. Bush, *Behind the Lines: East London Labour 1914–1919* (Merlin, 1984)

32 A. Davin, 'Imperialism and Motherhood', *History Workshop Journal*, 5, Spring 1978

33 P. Dewey, 'Military Recruiting and the British Labour Force During the First World War', *Historical Journal*, xxvii, 1984

34 D. Dwork, *War is Good for Babies and other Young Children: A History of the Infant and Child Welfare Movement in England, 1898–1918* (Tavistock, 1986)

35 D. Englander, 'Die Demobilmachung in Grossbritannien nach dem Ersten Weltkrieg', *Geschichte und Gesellschaft*, ix, 1983

36 D. Englander and J. Osborne, 'Jack, Tommy and Henry Dubb: the Armed Forces and the British Working Class', *Historical Journal*, xxi, 1978

37 R. C. K. Ensor, *England 1870–1914* (Oxford University Press, 1936)

38 B. B. Gilbert, *British Social Policy, 1914–1939* (Batsford, 1970)

39 S. R. Graubard, 'Military Demobilisation in Britain following the First World War', *Journal of Modern History*, xix, 1947

40 K. Grieves, *The Politics of Manpower, 1914–18* (Manchester University Press, 1988)

41 E. Halevy, *History of the English People in the Nineteenth Century*, Vol. 5, *Imperialism and the Rise of Labour, 1895–1905* (Benn, 1929)

42 P. B. Johnson, *Land Fit for Heroes: the Planning of British Reconstruction, 1916–19* (Chicago University Press, 1968)

43 M. Langan and B. Schwartz, *Crises in the British State 1880–1930* (Hutchinson, 1985)

44 R. Lowe, 'The Erosion of State Intervention in Britain, 1917–1924', *Economic History Review*, 2nd Series, xxxi, 2, 1978

45 A. Marwick, *The Deluge: British Society and the First World War* (Bodley Head, 1965)

46 A. Marwick, 'The Impact of the First World War on Britain', *Journal of Contemporary History*, iii, 1, 1968

47 A. Marwick, *Women at War 1914–1918* (Fontana, 1977)

48 R. C. G. Matthew, R. McKibbon and J. A. Kay, 'The Franchise Factor in the Rise of the Labour Party', *English Historical Review*, xci, 1976

49 K. D. Morgan, *Consensus and Disunity: the Lloyd George Coalition Government, 1918–22* (Oxford University Press, 1979)

50 C. L. Mowat, *Britain Between the Wars* (Methuen, 1955)

51 P. Panayi, *The Enemy Within: Germans in Britain During the First World War* (Berg, 1990)

52 H. Pelling, 'British Labour and British Imperialism', *Popular Politics and Society in Late Victorian Britain* (Macmillan, 1968 edn.)

53 R. Pope, 'Adjustment to Peace: Educational Provision for Unemployed Juveniles, 1918–19', *British Journal of Education Studies*, xxvii, 1, 1979

54 R. Price, *An Imperial War and the British Working Class* (Routledge and Kegan Paul, 1972)

55 M. Pugh, 'Politicians and the Woman's Vote, 1914–1918', *History*, lix, 1974

56 N. Reeves, *Official British Film Propaganda During the First World War* (Croom Helm, 1986)

57 M. Rose, 'The Success of Social Reform? The Central Control Board (Liquor Traffic) 1915–21' in M. R. D. Foot (ed.), *War and Society* (Elek, 1973)

58 A. Rothstein, *The Soldiers' Strikes of 1919* (Macmillan, 1980)

59 G. Sherrington, *English Education, Social Change and War 1911–20*

(Manchester University Press, 1981)

60 P. Simkins, *Kitchener's Army. The Raising of the New Armies, 1914–16* (Manchester University Press, 1988)

61 B. Simon, *Education and the Labour Movement, 1870–1920* (Lawrence and Wishart, 1965)

62 B. Simon, *The Politics of Educational Reform, 1920–1940* (Lawrence and Wishart, 1974)

63 E. Spiers, *The Army and Society, 1815–1914* (Longman, 1980)

64 M. Swenarton, *Homes Fit for Heroes* (Heinemann, 1981)

65 R. H. Tawney, 'The Abolition of Economic Controls, 1918–21', *Economic History Review*, 1st Series, xii, 1943

66 B. Waites, *A Class Society at War, England 1914–18* (Berg, 1987)

67 T. Wilson, *The Downfall of the Liberal Party, 1914–1935* (Collins, 1968)

68 T. Wilson, *The Myriad Faces of War: Britain and the Great War 1914–18* (Polity, 1986)

69 J. Winter, *Socialism and the Challenge of War* (Routledge and Kegan Paul, 1974)

70 J. Winter, 'The Impact of the First World War on Civilian Health in Britain', *Economic History Review*, 2nd Series, xxx, 3, 1977

71 J. Winter, 'Military Fitness and Public Health in Britain During the First World War', *Journal of Contemporary History*, xv, 1980

72 J. Winter, *The Great War and the British People* (Macmillan, 1985)

73 J. Winter, *The Experience of World War I* (Guild, 1988)

Primary sources

74 Christopher Addison, *Four and a Half Years*, vols I and II (Hutchinson, 1934)

75 Vera Brittain, *Testament of Youth* (Gollancz, 1933)

76 W. S. Churchill, *The Aftermath* (Macmillan, 1941 edn.)

77 S. Pankhurst, *The Home Front* (Hutchinson, 1932)

78 R. Roberts, *The Classic Slum* (Manchester University Press, 1971)

79 R. H. Tawney, 'Keep the Workers' Children in their Place', (*Daily News* 14.2.18) reprinted in *The Radical Tradition* (Allen and Unwin, 1964)

WORKS DEALING WITH THE SECOND WORLD WAR

80 P. Addison, *The Road to 1945* (Cape, 1975)

81 P. Addison, *Now the War is Over* (BBC/Cape, 1985)
82 C. Barnett, *The Audit of War* (Macmillan, 1986)
83 G. M. Beck, *Survey of British Employment and Unemployment, 1927–1951* (Oxford University, Dept of Statistics, 1951)
84 A. Booth, 'The "Keynesian Revolution" in Economic Policy-making', *Economic History Review*, 2nd Series, xxxvi, 1983
85 A. Booth, 'Defining a Keynesian Revolution', *Economic History Review*, xxxvii, 2, 1984
86 A. Briggs, *A History of Broadcasting in the United Kingdom*, Vol. 3, *A War of Words* (Oxford University Press, 1970)
87 A. Bullock, *The Life and Times of Ernest Bevin*, Vol. 2, *Minister of Labour* (Heinemann, 1967)
88 A. Cairncross, *Years of Recovery* (Methuen, 1985)
89 A. Calder, *The People's War, 1939–45* (Cape, 1969)
90 P. Calvocoressi and G. Wint, *Total War* (Allen Lane, 1972)
91 T. C. Crosby, *The Impact of Civilian Evacuation in the Second World War* (Croom Helm, 1986)
92 R. Croucher, *Engineers at War, 1939–1945* (Merlin, 1982)
93 J. C. R. Dow, *The Management of the British Economy, 1945–60* (Cambridge University Press)
94 R. Eatwell, *The 1945–1951 Labour Governments* (Batsford, 1979)
95 D. Englander and A. Mason, *The British Soldier in World War II* (Warwick Working Paper in Social History, n.d.)
96 M. Foot, *Aneurin Bevan, 1945–1960* (Davis Poynter, 1963)
97 P. Fussell, *Wartime* (Oxford University Press, 1989)
98 P. H. J. H. Gosden, *Education in the Second World War* (Methuen, 1976)
99 M. Gowing, 'The Organisation of Manpower in Britain during the Second World War', *Journal of Contemporary History*, vii, 1972
100 W. Harrington and P. Young, *The 1945 Revolution* (Davis Poynter, 1978)
101 J. Harris, 'Social Policy-making in Britain during the Second World War', W. Mommsen (ed.) *The Emergence of the Welfare State in Britain and Germany* (Croom Helm, 1981)
102 P. Inman, *Labour in the Munitions Industries* (HMSO, 1957)
103 B. S. Johnson, *The Evacuees* (Gollancz, 1968)
104 P. Lewis, *A People's War* (Thames Methuen/Channel 4, 1986)
105 R. B. McCallum and A. Readman, *The General Election of 1945* (Oxford University Press, 1947)
106 I. McClaine, *Ministry of Morale: Home Front Morale and the Ministry of Information in World War II* (Allen and Unwin, 1979)

107 J. Macnicol, *The Movement for Family Allowances, 1918–45* (Heinemann, 1980)

108 A. Marwick, 'People's War and Top People's Peace', in A. Sked and C. Cook (eds), *Crisis and Controversy: Essays in Honour of A. J. P. Taylor* (Macmillan, 1976)

109 A. Marwick, *The Home Front* (Thames and Hudson, 1976)

110 R. C. O. Matthews, 'Why Britain has had Full Employment since the War', *Economic Journal*, lxvii, 1968

111 R. Minns, *Bangers and Mash: The Domestic Front, 1939–45* (Virago, 1980)

112 K. O. Morgan, *Labour in Power* (Oxford University Press, 1984)

113 H. M. D. Parker, *Manpower* (HMSO, 1957)

114 H. Pelling, 'The 1945 General Election Result Reconsidered; *Historical Journal*, xxiii, 1980

115 H. Pelling, *The Labour Governments 1945–51* (Macmillan, 1984)

116 R. Pope, 'The Planning and Implementation of British Demobilisation, 1941–46' (unpublished Ph.D. thesis, Open University, 1986)

117 A. Pratt, 'The Labour Party and Family Income Support Policy, 1940–1979' (unpublished Ph.D. thesis, Bradford University, 1988)

118 D. Riley, '"The Free Mothers". Pro-natalism and Working Women in Industry at the end of the Last War in Britain', *History Workshop Journal*, 11, Spring 1981

119 M. Sissons and P. French (eds), *The Age of Austerity, 1945–1951* (Hodder and Stoughton, 1963)

120 H. Smith, 'The Problem of Equal Pay for Equal Work in Great Britain during World War II', *Journal of Modern History*, liv, 1982

121 H. Smith (ed.), *War and Social Change: British Society in the Second World War* (Manchester University Press, 1986)

122 N. Stammers, *Civil Liberties in Britain during the Second World War* (Croom Helm, 1983)

123 P. Summerfield, *Women Workers in the Second World War* (Croom Helm, 1984)

124 R. M. Titmuss, *Problems of Social Policy* (HMSO, 1950)

125 J. D. Tomlinson, 'Why was there never a "Keynesian Revolution" in economic policy?', *Economy and Society*, 10, 1981

126 J. D. Tomlinson, 'A "Keynesian Revolution" in Economic

Policy-making', *Economic History Review*, 2nd Series, xxxvii, 2

127 G. Wright, *The Ordeal of Total War, 1939–1945* (Harper and Row, 1968)

Primary sources

128 V. Brittain, *Testament of Experience* (Gollancz, 1957)
129 R. Broad and S. Fleming (eds), *Nella Last's War* (Sphere edn., 1983)
130 R. A. Butler, *The Art of the Possible* (Hamish Hamilton, 1971)
131 M. Cole, *Wartime Billeting* (Fabian Society/Gollancz, 1941)
132 M. Cole, *The Rate for the Job* (Fabian Society/Gollancz, 1946)
133 H. Dalton, *High Tide and After: Memoirs 1945–1960* (Muller, 1962)
134 T. Harrison, *Living Through the Blitz* (Collins, 1976)
135 Mass-Observation, *People in Production* (John Murray, 1942)
136 Mass-Observation, *War Factory* (Gollancz, 1943)
137 Mass-Observation, *The Journey Home* (Advertising Services Guild, 1944)
138 S. Orwell and I. Angus (eds), *The Collected Essays, Journalism and Letters of George Orwell*, Vol. II, *My Country Right or Left 1940–1943* (Secker and Warburg, 1968)
139 B. Pimlott (ed.), *The Second World War Diary of Hugh Dalton, 1940–45* (Cape, 1986)
140 J. B. Priestley, *Postscripts* (Heinemann, 1940)
141 Royal Commission on Equal Pay, *Report*, Cmd 6957 (HMSO, 1946)
142 G. Thomas, *Wartime Social Survey: Women at Work* (HMSO, 1944)
143 G. Thomas, *Women in Industry* (HMSO, 1949)

Index

Index